FENTRESS BRADBURN

Selected and Current Works

FENTRESS BRADBURN

Selected and Current Works

First published in Australia in 1998 by
The Images Publishing Group Pty Ltd
ACN 059 734 431
6 Bastow Place, Mulgrave, Victoria, 3170
Telephone (61 3) 9561 5544 Facsimile (61 3) 9561 4860

National Library of Australia Cataloguing-in-Publication Data

Fentress Bradburn: selected and current works.

Bibliography.
Includes index.
ISBN 1 875498 86 9.

1. Fentress Bradburn (Firm). 2. Architecture, Modern—20th
century—United States. 3. Architecture, American. I. Fentress Bradburn
(Firm). (Series: Master architect series).

720.973

Edited by Stephen Dobney
Designed by The Graphic Image Studio Pty Ltd,
Mulgrave, Australia
Film by Scanagraphix Australia Pty Ltd
Printed in Hong Kong

Contents

INTRODUCTION

Introduction

Fentress Bradburn Architects

After graduating from North Carolina State University's School of Design in 1972, Curtis Worth Fentress went to work in New York, first in the office of I.M. Pei, then with the newly formed firm of Kohn Pedersen Fox (KPF). Pei's Modernism and KPF's explorations in Post-Modernism would influence Fentress's work; however, his belief in the importance of humanism in architecture would add a more powerful dimension. He would go on to develop a unique form of architectural expression with the ultimate goal of creating humanly attainable structures with a profound sense of place.

Fentress was able to explore his theories and their applications further when he formed his own firm in Denver, Colorado, in 1980. He was joined in his efforts by James Henry Bradburn. Bradburn, a graduate of Rensselaer Polytechnic Institute, had cultivated a flair for innovative technical solutions during his tenure with Kevin Roche John Dinkeloo and Associates. A protege of Dinkeloo, Bradburn garnered strong knowledge of production technology from his mentor, and gained a love of applying innovative construction techniques to design.

The success of the firm stems from its ability to meld two distinctly separate, but interdependent, facets of architecture: art and science. Artistic concepts are the realm of Mr Fentress, the firm's principal in charge of design. Addressing each project in a unique and relevant way, his designs impart something of a local region's past, as well as something of the larger, global context of the future. Mr Bradburn, principal in charge of production, grounds these visions in reality, making the concepts physically possible. An architect with the heart of an engineer, he allows the latest technical aspects of contemporary architecture to be achieved through the rigors of engineering and science.

Maintaining the careful balance between art and science, Fentress Bradburn has developed not an architectural style, but rather a style of architecture. This is neither a conglomeration of styles nor a conscious avoidance of styles, but the emergence of something altogether new. Their projects are a testament to the fact that artistry and technology can coexist with an appreciation for human needs and a respect for context. It is an idea that owes more to the figure at the center of da Vinci's "Vitruvian Man" than to the geometries derived from it.

When an architect's work is considered, its theoretical foundations are often discussed as much as the built form itself. Our firm welcomes such consideration, as it offers a great deal of insight into our design process. Focusing on humanism, we seek to fulfill simple ideas of physical comfort. To us, as architects, this desire springs from the very heart of humanist thought—we are designing for people. Our work is about making people comfortable, not about the merely abstract expression of a technological future. Rather than debating the merits of design as its own end or rehashing past discussions about architectural "styles", we established the distinct character that would define our work—the human equation. Our buildings would consider the physical and psychological comfort of the end-user—the people who live and work in and around them.

To strengthen the human sense of our buildings, we incorporate elements that are identifiable within their specific region, including major landmarks, historical events, and peoples. We began to understand that seeking out the imagery of the built environment was not enough, so we sought further. Looking to a site's natural physical features, we considered landscape, environment, ecology, and topography. We went on to examine how an area's history, culture, memory, and myth might be evoked through the built form. Sometimes our interpretation of cultural and historical references and elements of nature results in solutions that operate on metaphor, symbol, and even myth. These abstract concepts exist in the realm of theory; making them material is our on-going challenge. The approach we developed unearths the combination of elements that define a site, and thus our building upon it. We termed our approach "contextual regionalism", defined by *Architecture* magazine as "designing for a place".

Early on, our desire to create a more contextually oriented building led to such technological innovations as the mirrored curtain wall of 116 Inverness Drive East. This was followed by the 50-story Reliance Tower. Other innovations soon followed, such as a structural post-tensioned limestone spandrel created for the Terrace Towers Complex, which began construction in 1981. This technology was expanded upon and rose to 45 stories on 1999 Broadway.

Also for 1999 Broadway, we utilized several methods to help integrate qualities such as comfort, visual clarity, accessibility, and approachability into our design. We actually lifted the high-rise tower off the ground on giant columns, creating a park underneath with landscaped areas in which to rest, eat lunch, or just relax. This creates a contemplative zone around a historic church that visually cushions it from the busy city.

Our commitment to values and strong design led us to victory in the 1987 Colorado Convention Center competition. This project lent Fentress Bradburn a solid presence. The brief for the Colorado Convention Center included a lengthy list of requirements which we simplified by employing theoretical humanism as a design methodology. One of the principal challenges was to create a dialogue between the firm and the public—the ultimate users of the project. We attended more than 100 meetings with citizens, meeting planners, private interest groups, and at least 40 user groups to formalize the requirements and concerns that would provide the basis for the overall design. Beyond purely organizational and programmatic concerns, these groups indicated that the building must be easy to understand and navigate. Restrooms needed to be designed for real functionality, with the ability to accommodate the sometimes large crowds at conventions and events; the building had to have windows, and fit comfortably into the urban fabric of downtown Denver. These requests generated important elements of the final design. Conference areas are numbered consecutively (not named) and are arranged in close proximity to each other. The partitions between adjacent men's and women's restrooms can be moved, making them better able to serve specific conference crowds. As the program stipulated that no windows were to be inserted in the body of the building, our design team increased the fenestration at the major entrances, breaking the "box" of the center proper and creating a communication corridor that extends from the interior outward into the city and the mountain scenery beyond.

One of the most notable projects that followed was the internationally acclaimed Denver International Airport. It is truly a project which embodies the ethos of Fentress Bradburn. A powerful sense of place is evoked by the airport's peaked roof design, which pays homage to the undulating silhouette of the nearby Rocky Mountains. Technological innovations abound in the terminal roof's construction, not only in the engineering of the Teflon-coated tensile membrane, but also in the way it is used to fully enclose a space rather than acting merely as a canopy. The terminal's Great Hall is vast, with a grandeur that recalls the awe which travel once inspired, but the daylight that enters the space through its fabric roof bathes the area in a comforting, approachable familiarity. The pleasant interior space benefits the physical and psychological well-being of employees and travelers alike.

The Jefferson County Government Center Courts and Administration Building is designed for the ease and security of all its users (public, inmates, and staff). With its integration of exterior and interior and its general openness, it reflects the Jeffersonian ideal of open and accessible government. The entry atrium is a centering device which, coupled with the radial arms, adds focus, clarity, and stability without cloistering. The psychological integration of exterior and interior, particularly the exterior hallways, alleviates many of the common stresses associated with the functions of a courts and administrative building.

The new administrative complex in Oakland, California, takes the idea of the contemplative zone and extrapolates it to create a large and uninterrupted urban piazza. This open space serves as the central focus for the weaving together of Oakland's historical fabric with its new additions and pedestrian linkages to important urban terminus points. In this composition, we have created a landmark from an otherwise confusing confluence of streets and avenues. Thus, the historical memory of the place is enhanced and the community spirit and pride of Oakland is re-energized.

Clark County's Government Center in Clark County, Nevada, is a symbol of the county's natural environment. The notions of centering and clarity of direction are expressed here by a strong organizational spine that intersects the master plan. A series of buildings are arranged along this spine, each designed in hierarchical scale to its neighbor. An armature of trees and a gradually shortening wall come together on the county courtyard to enclose an open-air amphitheater. Social and ecological concerns demanded an emphasis on preservation and efficient utilization of natural and local resources. In response to Nevada's desert and people, we designed punched windows set in thick walls to reduce heat loss and gain. Using local materials enhanced both the natural surroundings and the contextual connection of the inhabitants.

The National Cowboy Hall of Fame in Oklahoma City, Oklahoma, presented several challenges. In order to correct many of the problems with the existing structure and enlarge it to four times its original size, a sensitivity to the institution and its founders was required. A new entry and linking hall was devised to welcome the visitor and evoke the heroic aura of the cowboy and the American West. Two new wings and a fountain courtyard create a hospitable sense of place for the complex.

The National Museum of Wildlife Art is the definitive expression of our ecological sensitivity. It emerges from a cliffside in Jackson, Wyoming, as a natural stone outcropping, worked into the landscape by the use of native materials. The building reveals itself slowly from its winding promenade and creates a true sense of discovery for the visitor. In its compositional subtlety of emergence and recession, it grows out of the landscape while drawing in and enclosing the patron.

In all of our projects, the human equation is paramount as a consideration for everything from scale and light to interior layout and design. We strive to create and utilize open space, incorporate local materials, introduce natural light, and clarify movement to make even the most monumental buildings comfortable and humanly accessible. Our concern for humanism and our interest in place continue to drive our designs.

SELECTED AND CURRENT WORKS

One Mile High Plaza

Design 1980
Denver, Colorado
J. Roulier Interests, Developer
947,000 square feet
Composite steel frame, concrete core
Stainless steel, granite

Fentress Bradburn was commissioned to build a 40-story corporate office tower on a prime site in lower downtown Denver, Colorado.

One Mile High Plaza was designed to be an elegantly intriguing landmark in the Denver cityscape. The design for this multifaceted building was inspired by the image of a vein of mineral ore exposed in a rock crevasse. The entrance features a glass-covered cascading atrium that continues the upper level motif of the building's crystalline facade. In front of the atrium is a broad and expansive plaza.

One Mile High Plaza's underlying design philosophy addresses the site's contextual requirements, both natural (sun, wind and topography) and man-made (urban, contrived and built). In response to the natural context, the cladding of granite and glass blends with the natural elements of the surrounding landscape. In response to the man-made context, this cladding lessens the tower's visual impact on the surrounding urban fabric, and the building as a whole is a carefully studied re-evaluation of urban building design and its general approach to energy use.

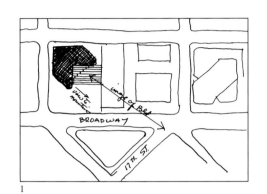

1

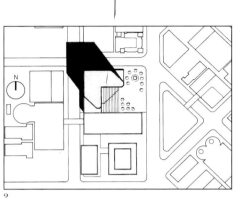

2

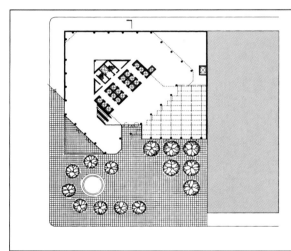

3

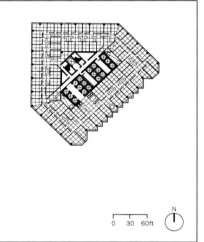

4

5

6

1 Location sketch
2 Site plan
3 Broadway level plan and typical single-tenant floor plan
4 Interior of galleria
5 Model showing plaza
6 Model perspective
7 Model of entry lobby
8 Plaza model
9 Rendered perspective
10 Perspective view
11 South elevation

7

8

9

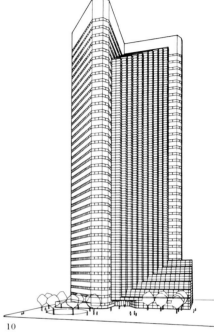

10

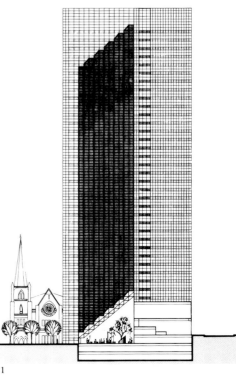

11

Terrace Towers Master Plan

Design 1980
Englewood, Colorado
J. Roulier Interests
7,000,000 square feet

The Terrace Towers Master Plan is
a mixed-use project set on a 48-acre site.
The plan is for a 20-year phased
development consisting of two clusters
of four buildings linked by a pedestrian
spine housing retail, fast-food cafes and
restaurants, with adjacent parking
facilities.

The eight towers make a unique
architectural statement in form, height
and shape. The beveled corners and
indented sides that break up the mass
of each tower create an illusion of four
smaller, clustered towers, thus reducing
the visual weight of the buildings while
still projecting a sense of corporate
dynamism.

Four structures have been completed to
date: Milestone Tower, Terrace Tower II
and two detached parking structures.
When complete, the Terrace Towers
development is expected to become
a focal point for the expansive Denver
Technological Center.

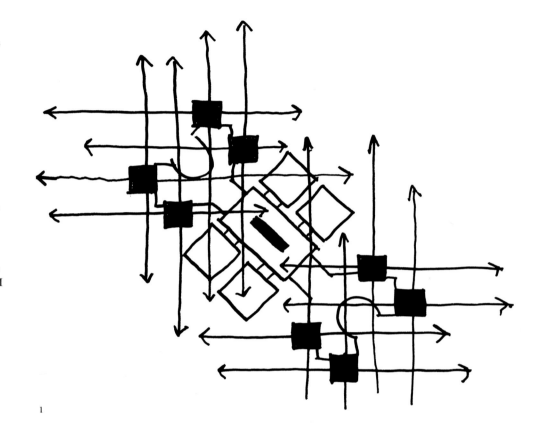

1

2

18

1 Concept sketch
2 Model photo
3 Aerial view of model

3

Milestone Tower Headquarters

Design/Completion 1980/1982
Englewood, Colorado
J. Roulier Interests, Developer
240,000 square feet
Composite steel frame, concrete core
Limestone, glass, granite

The principal building of the Terrace
Towers Master Plan is Milestone Tower,
the headquarters of Milestone Petroleum.
This 12-story Indiana limestone building
is designed as four stacked and terraced
modules, with chamfered corners and
indentions at the facade midpoints
creating a double octagon. This shape is
emphasized in the lobby by an octagonal
staircase opening that leads down to
a retail concourse one floor below.
At the top of the terrace of the building,
a landscaped dining area overlooks the
Denver skyline and its mountain
panorama.

In this project, the firm advanced current
building technology by developing a post-
tensioned limestone spandrel beam to
carry the facade glazing. This was the
first project in the world to use such
a technique.

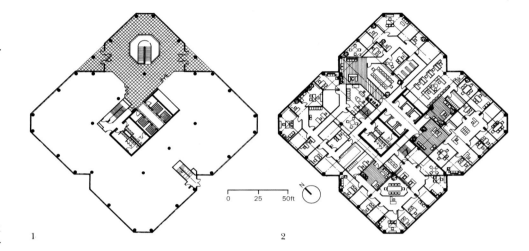

1

2

1   Ground floor plan
2   Typical floor plan
3   Exterior view
Opposite:
    Exterior view across park
Following page:
    Model view

3

20

Tele-Communications Inc. Headquarters
Terrace Tower II

Design/Completion 1983/1985
Englewood, Colorado
J. Roulier Interests, Developer
240,000 square feet
Composite steel frame, concrete core
Limestone, glass, granite

While being visually identical to its twin, Milestone Tower, TCI Headquarters nonetheless offered Fentress Bradburn a unique opportunity to revisit the original design and to upgrade and improve it. Subtle differences are seen in the environmental control systems and related computer advancements. Additional modifications were made to provide suitable headquarters accommodation for the telecommunications giant.

This is the second tower in the planned four-tower node which will serve as a business center at the western end of the site. To the east, a second collection of towers will eventually be built to house office and hotel functions. The entire complex will be tied together by a spine of retail shops and restaurants.

1

1   Parking structure
2   Exterior elevation

2

116 Inverness Drive East

Design/Completion 1981/1982
Englewood, Colorado
116 Inverness, Central Development Group
230,000 square feet
Composite steel frame. concrete core
Monolithic and insulating glass, slate, stainless steel

Located at the main entrance to an 840-acre park, 116 Inverness Drive East sits on a hillside overlooking the championship 18-hole Inverness Golf Course and the Rocky Mountains to the west. In plan, the design is a double X anchored by a central, three-story diamond-shaped atrium.

The desire to locate the building on the rolling hills east of the mountains made two tasks paramount: reducing the visual weight of the building and preserving views from the maximum number of office spaces. To reduce its visual weight, the building is clad in alternating bands of green vision glass and silver spandrel glass. The sleek, reflective-glass building either glistens in the sunlight or blends with its natural surroundings in overcast conditions. Balconies are positioned above the two wings facing the mountains to take maximum advantage of views from the site. The building's interlocking configuration also makes the best use of perimeter and corner office spaces.

This design was the first in the Rocky Mountain region to use a four-sided, structural silicone glazing system and among the first in the world to combine this technique with insulating vision glass to create a monolithic surface.

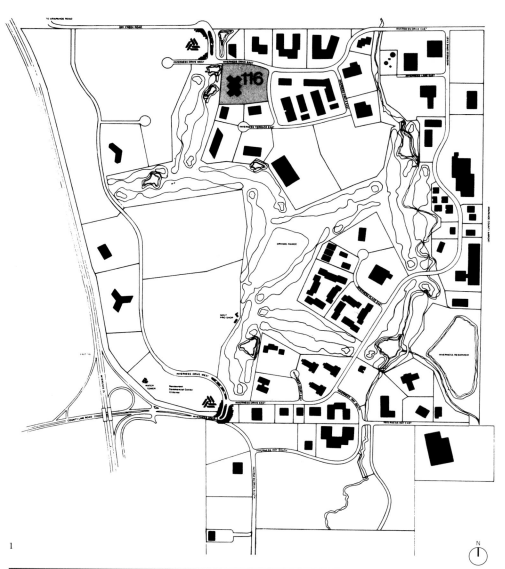

1

2

3

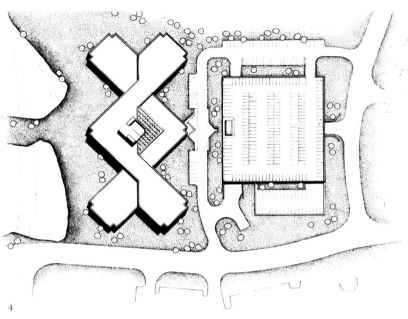

4

5

6

7

8

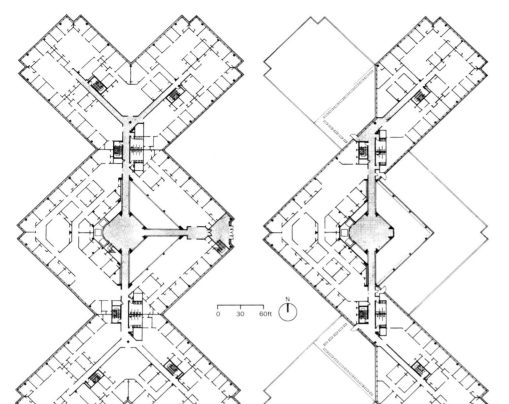

9

10

11

12

1999 Broadway

Design/Completion 1981/1985
Denver, Colorado
First Interstate Structures Inc.
760,000 square feet
Composite steel frame, concrete core
Limestone, glass, granite, marble

1999 Broadway stands on a triangular site in the central business district of Denver, a site which it shares with an American eclectic and Neo-Renaissance church built in 1924. Rather than overwhelming the historic parish church, the new tower is designed to enhance the siting of this religious landmark, offering a unique juxtaposition of sanctuary and skyscraper. Although separated by 60 years of architectural design and divergent purposes, the two buildings complement each other due to Fentress Bradburn's carefully integrated architectural design.

The columns on which the tower rests create a tall, stepped arcade that allows the church to remain physically independent and visually open. The resulting space offers complete circulation around both the church and the tower and creates two landscaped plazas for rest and contemplation. One of these plazas, paved in gray-green granite, features an undulating wall with built-in seating to conceal the down ramp to the underground parking facilities. The other is landscaped with trees surrounded by granite boxes to provide extra seating.

Facing the center of the site, 1999 Broadway has a concave wall of reflective glass that cradles and dramatizes the sculptural form of the church. Generated from an arithmetic spiral, the multifaceted curtain wall literally wraps around the older building. On its opposite face, the tower's sharp corner projects into the city's central business district, presenting a strong, contemporary image. Thus, the impression of the power of enterprise invoked by the spire of this corporate tower is juxtaposed with the equally imposing symbol of strength represented by the church steeple. The peaceful coexistence of the sanctuary and the skyscraper proves that architecture can be used to save existing historic landmarks while simultaneously fulfilling the requirements of modern commercial development.

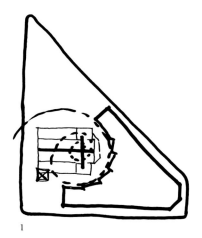

1

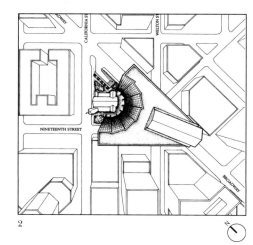

2

3

4

5

6

1   Concept sketch
2   Site plan
3   Exterior view in the afternoon
4   Detail
5   California Street plaza
6   Broadway entrance
7   19th Street public plaza

7

8   Ground floor plan
9   Mid-rise level plan
10   High-rise level plan
Opposite:
     Exterior at dawn in winter

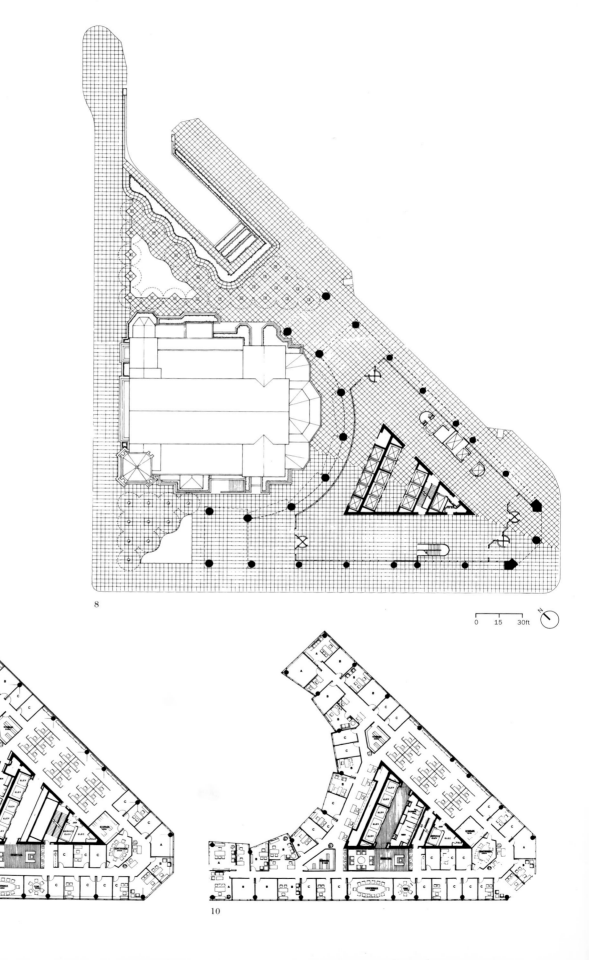

8

0   15   30ft

9

10

13

14

15

16

17   Interior from elevator towards lobby
Opposite:
    Elevator lobby

17

Reliance Tower

Design 1982
Denver, Colorado
Reliance Development
1,400,000 square feet
Composite steel frame, concrete core
Glass, granite

Fentress Bradburn's plan for the Reliance Tower, located on I.M. Pei's 16th Street Pedestrian Mall in downtown Denver, abandons the columnar rigidity of the classic American skyscraper. The base projects outward from the shaft of the tower to create an elegant plaza designed to bring the building's monumental proportions down to a more human scale.

The obverse side of the building is sheathed in monolithic mullionless glazing in a continuous glass wall that appears as a monumental cinematic reflection of city activity seen against Denver's mountain panorama. This 270-foot-wide, curvilinear, reflective silver-gray surface is an integrated unit of four-sided structural silicone and glass, which was first explored by the firm on 116 Inverness Drive East.

Reliance Tower was the tallest building on the Denver skyline at the time of its design.

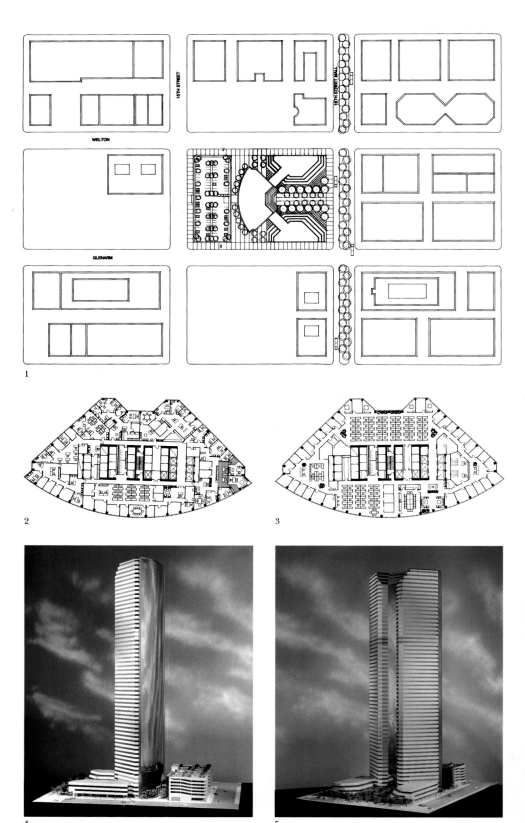

1

2

3

4

5

6

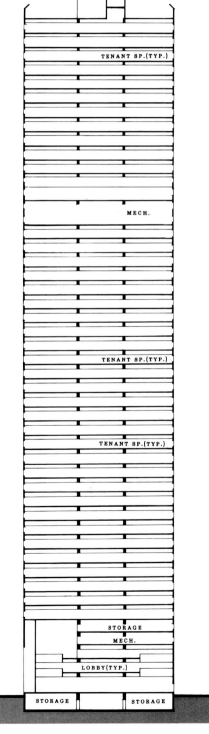

TENANT SP.(TYP.)

MECH.

TENANT SP.(TYP.)

TENANT SP.(TYP.)

STORAGE
MECH.

LOBBY(TYP.)

STORAGE   STORAGE

7

Reliance Tower 37

One DTC

Design/Completion 1983/1985
Englewood, Colorado
Murray Properties of Colorado
230,000 square feet
Composite steel frame, concrete core
Granite, stainless steel

Located in the 900-acre Denver Technological Center on Denver's southern edge, One DTC is notable for the way it incorporates materials and design to create timeless beauty and enduring quality in a user-friendly space. The orientation and elevation of the building, as well as the location of the parking structure, serve as a buffer to noise from the adjacent freeway. The openness and sculptured beauty of the plaza introduce the lobby in a grand yet personal manner. The structure's symbiosis with the surrounding environment creates a thoroughly efficient, yet totally humanized, business environment.

The rectangular plan of the high-rise has serrated edges on two diagonally opposite corners, thereby providing 80 percent of the offices with panoramic views. The 13-story building is raised on 30-foot columns to create a grand entry and *porte cochère* which link the building and parking structure. The columns serve to open up the site and connect the plaza to the Denver Technological Center's pedestrian walkway system. They also allow the building's mechanical systems to be located on the lower level of the parking garage, thereby maximizing the amount of usable floorspace.

The exterior's granite-clad horizontal bands smoothly delineate the floors and provide scale. This simple repeated motif maintains visual comfort and aids user orientation.

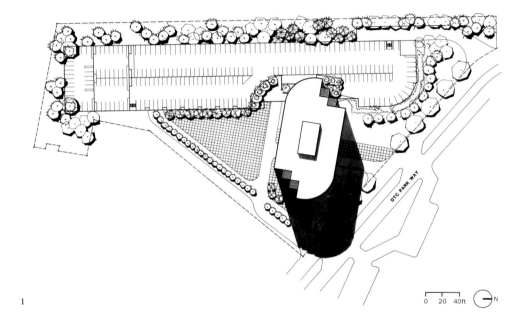

1

0 20 40ft   N

1 Site plan
2 Section
3 Elevated exterior perspective

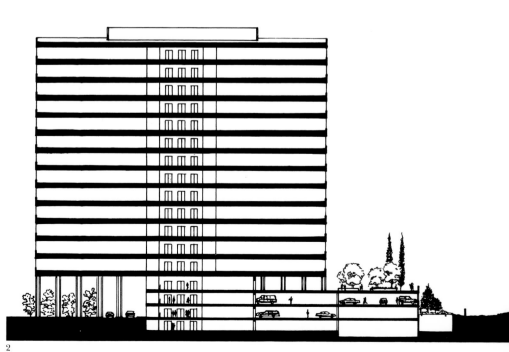

2

3

4

4 View from DTC Parkway
5 East view
6 Entry walk
7 Typical single-tenant floor plan
8 Typical multi-tenant floor plan
9 Eleventh floor plan (single tenant)

5

6

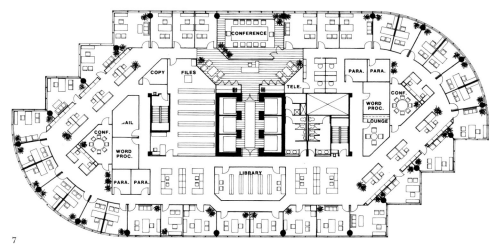

7

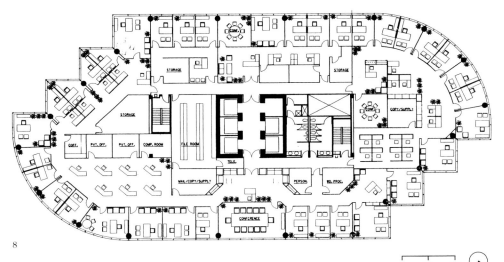

8

0   12   24ft

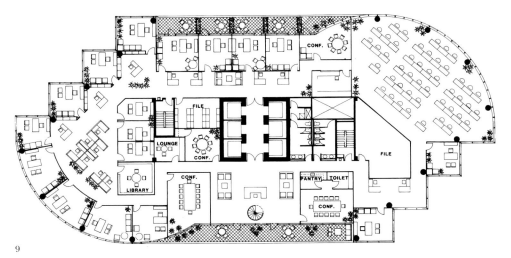

9

10 North elevation
11 *Porte cochère* entry area
12 Exterior column detail

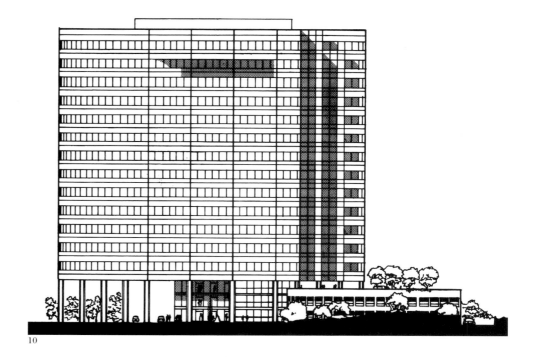

10

11

Norwest Tower

Design/Completion 1984/1986
Tucson, Arizona
Reliance Development Group
500,000 square feet
Composite steel frame, concrete core
Painted aluminum, granite, glass, bronze

Fentress Bradburn's showpiece in downtown Tucson is the 23-story Norwest Tower. The building is the first phase in a development program for this important site, which is viewed as the gateway to downtown Tucson's financial, governmental and cultural districts.

As an example of how a contemporary building can be integrated into its surroundings, it reflects the neighboring Spanish mission-style architecture with its tiers and domed cap. Through the design, the architects reinterpreted many of the city's icons and the surrounding natural environment. The tower's shaft echoes the paired spires of the adjacent Cathedral of Saint Augustine and its historical and regional cousin, San Xavier del Bac. The tower's hipped roof reflects the roof lines of territorial houses in the nearby Barrio Libre. Inside, the high-arched windows of the barrel-vaulted public lobby continue the tower's contextual allusions, reflecting the nearby Neo-Romanesque Bank One building.

A diagonal walkway bisects the site to link Tucson's financial district to its downtown cultural center. Bisecting the block in this way created a more interesting figure–field relationship, thus humanizing the space and avoiding the inappropriate and purely pragmatic solution of covering the whole site with building. Covered pedestrian arcades enclose two inviting public spaces which feature soft earth berms and grass. Each arcade is decorated with a central sculpture and periodically changed flags to enhance the sense of enclosure.

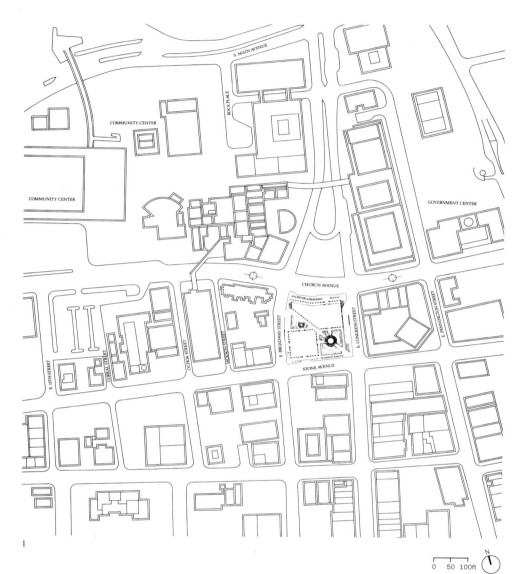

1

1   Neighborhood site plan
Opposite:
    View from park

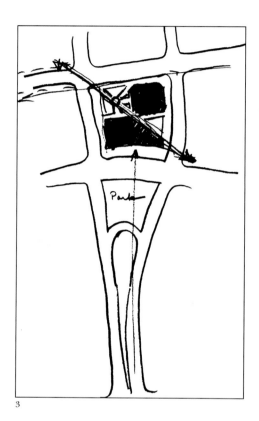

3

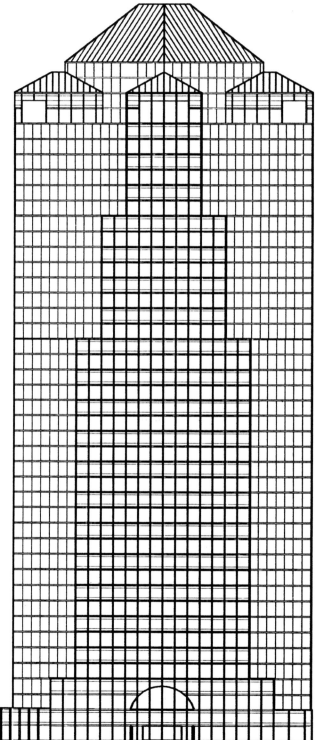

4

5

6

7

8

UNITED BANK OF ARIZONA

EXIT

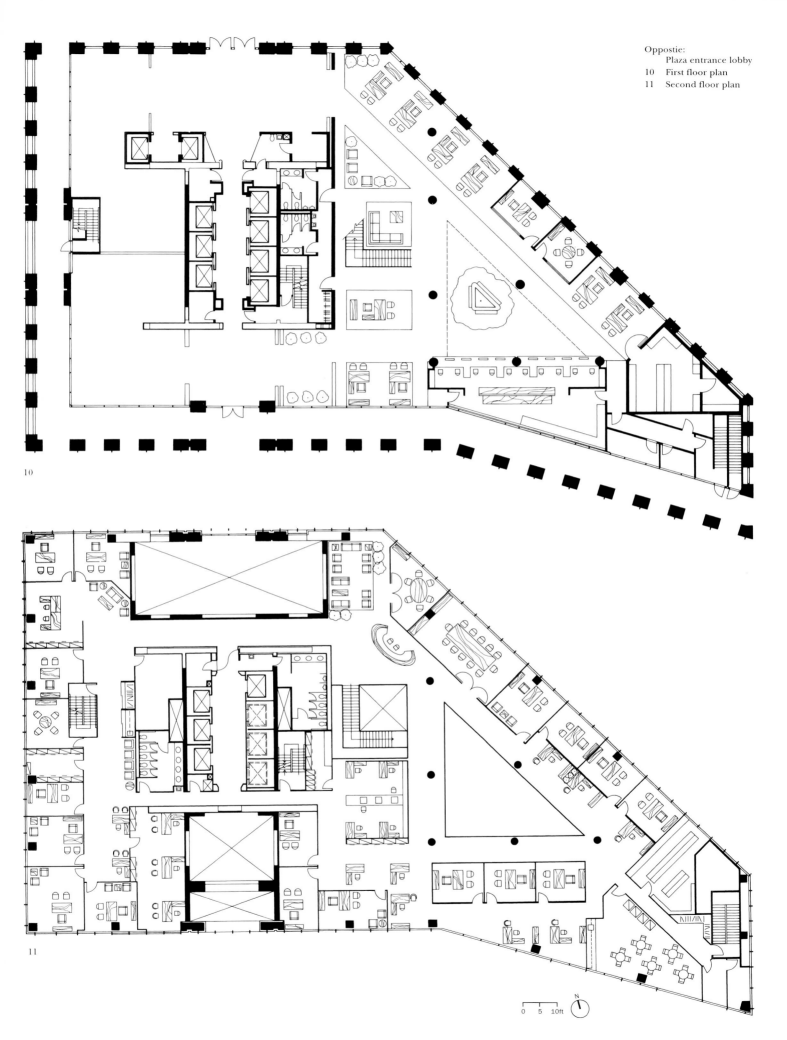

Oppostie:
Plaza entrance lobby
10 First floor plan
11 Second floor plan

10

11

0 5 10ft

12 Typical floor plan
13 Elevation
Opposite:
    Interior with skylights

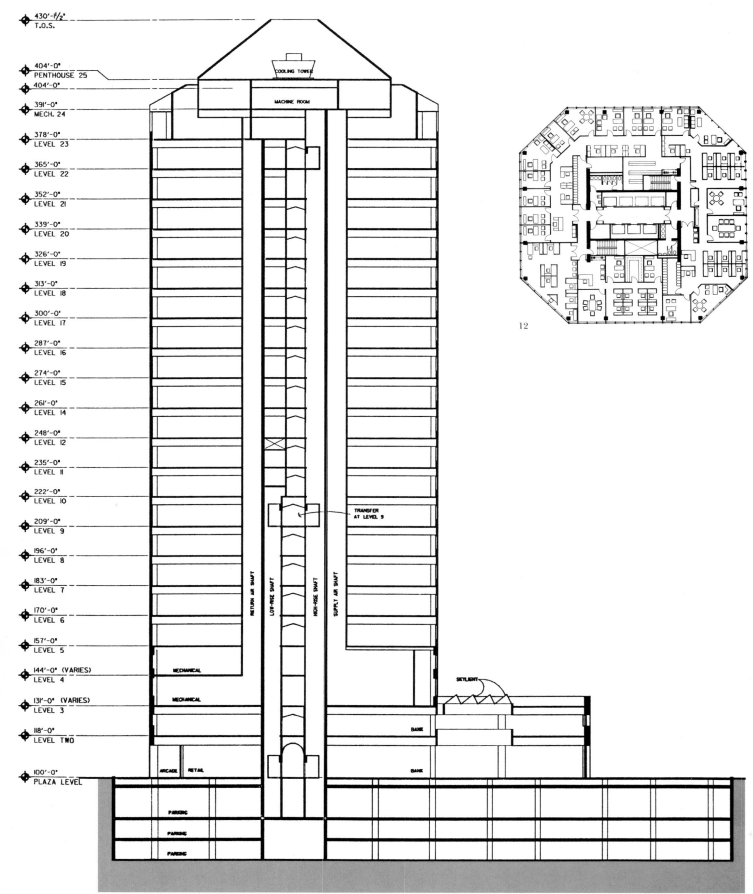

430'-1½"
T.O.S.

404'-0"
PENTHOUSE 25
404'-0"

391'-0"
MECH. 24

378'-0"
LEVEL 23

365'-0"
LEVEL 22

352'-0"
LEVEL 21

339'-0"
LEVEL 20

326'-0"
LEVEL 19

313'-0"
LEVEL 18

300'-0"
LEVEL 17

287'-0"
LEVEL 16

274'-0"
LEVEL 15

261'-0"
LEVEL 14

248'-0"
LEVEL 12

235'-0"
LEVEL 11

222'-0"
LEVEL 10

209'-0"
LEVEL 9

196'-0"
LEVEL 8

183'-0"
LEVEL 7

170'-0"
LEVEL 6

157'-0"
LEVEL 5

144'-0" (VARIES)
LEVEL 4

131'-0" (VARIES)
LEVEL 3

118'-0"
LEVEL TWO

100'-0"
PLAZA LEVEL

COOLING TOWER

MACHINE ROOM

RETURN AIR SHAFT

LOW-RISE SHAFT

HIGH-RISE SHAFT

SUPPLY AIR SHAFT

TRANSFER AT LEVEL 9

MECHANICAL

MECHANICAL

SKYLIGHT

BANK

BANK

ARCADE RETAIL

PARKING

PARKING

PARKING

12

13

Idaho Power Company Corporate Headquarters

Design/Completion 1986/1989
Boise, Idaho
Idaho Power Company
217,000 square feet
Composite steel frame, concrete core
Reinforced concrete, precast concrete, etched and honed
glass fiber reinforced concrete, granite, glass, travertine, bronze

The facade of a building is as important as its plan. The structure may be a sculptural object, but facade legibility is a fundamental key to understanding the comprehensive program. The facade of the Idaho Power Company describes a comforting and symmetrical enclosure. As the initial phase of a master plan for the Idaho Power Company Corporate Headquarters, this nine-story building is a stylistic marriage of Corbusian Classicism and mid-Modernism. The entrance is framed and identified by the interrelationship of its surrounding forms, its proportional fenestration and an encompassing Corbusian *brise-soleil*. Arranging the office tower like a column, from base to shaft to capital, further enhances the overall composition.

The first-phase headquarters building was to provide a focal point around which future developments could evolve. Structure and skin are object and subject, successfully fulfilling this objective.

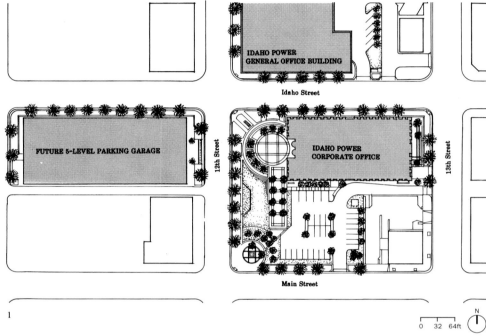

1

2

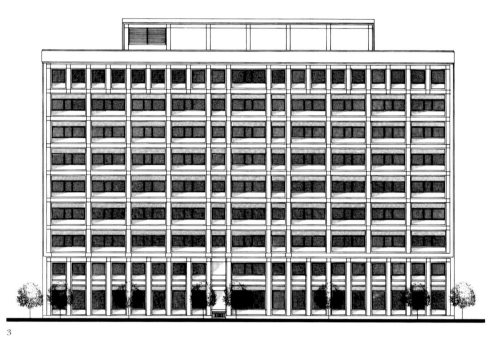

1   Site plan
2   12th Street elevation
3   North elevation
4   Main Street view
5   Main entrance plaza

3

4

5

6   Reception desk detail
7   Interior view
8   Ground floor plan
9   Typical floor plan
Opposite:
    Main lobby stair

6

7

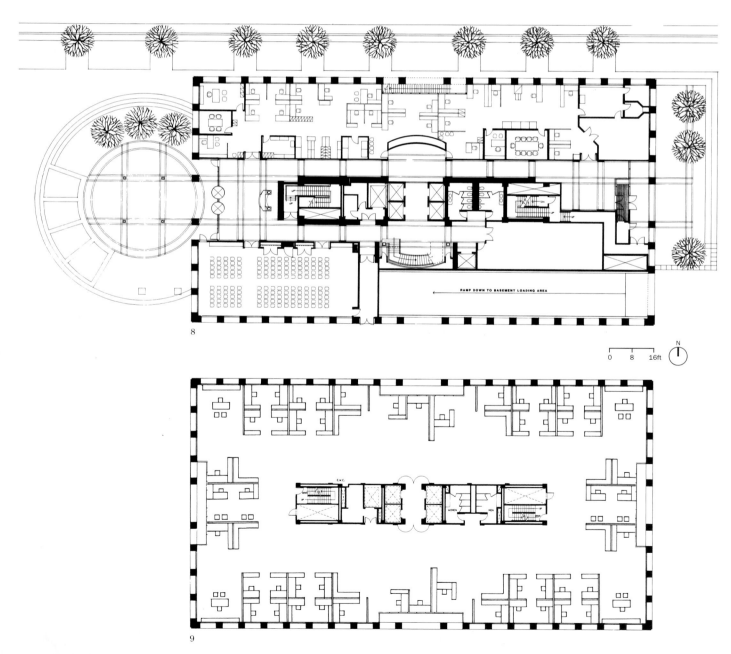

8

0   8   16ft

N

9

Jefferson County Government Center Master Plan

Design/Completion 1986/1989–92
Golden, Colorado
Jefferson County Colorado
1,000,000 square feet

As is the case with most localities which evolve out of or are influenced by a larger neighbor, Jefferson County, adjacent to Denver, had no recognizable center. Its functions had developed in a random fashion over a wide and demographically diverse region. Because of rapid population growth, Jefferson County had outgrown its infrastructure. The situation called for a new complex that would establish the symbolic importance of the county seat while creating a geographic center to generate an increased sense of community.

As the natural landscape is one of the county's recognized strengths, architecture and landscape had to be considered together. The site was linked to existing open space, trails and parks as well as new spaces which were incorporated as important elements in the design.

The complexities of civic functions and the rapid rate of population and economic growth in Jefferson County required that the design solution address the integration of new facilities for administration, justice, law enforcement, human resources, public parks and regulatory processing. The master plan also establishes new street patterns, landscaping, leisure facilities, picnic areas, amphitheaters and locations for future expansion.

1   Concept sketch
2   Master plan drawing
3   Master plan model

1

2

3

56

Jefferson County Human Services Building

Design/Completion 1986/1989
Golden, Colorado
Jefferson County Colorado
132,190 square feet
Composite steel frame, concrete core
Brick, glass, marble

The design of the Jefferson County Human Services Building seeks to show that civic architecture need not overwhelm to succeed. In fact, in some cases the reverse is true.

This building was given a human dimension by its welcoming, semi-circular, open-armed configuration. The four-story structure opens to a colonnaded plaza which encloses a landscaped courtyard. This acts as a transition between the building and the surrounding open space. The plaza is a semi-formal sculptural garden that provides a number of personal spaces and individual views of its sculptural elements. The transition space between this plaza and the purely functional spaces of the building sweeps upward from a single-story curtain wall to form a two-story skylit atrium corridor.

The building's psychological impact on its potential users was an important factor in the space planning of the Human Services Building. The building houses counseling, job training and placement, unemployment, day care and other services. Its spaces are designed to balance the complex need for privacy with the desire to be unconstrained. Instead of unfriendly barriers, carefully placed glass partitions achieve this balanced separation. Windows also play a key role by providing most rooms with an exterior view.

Continued

1

1   Distant view of building during winter
2   Sectional elevation through building centerline

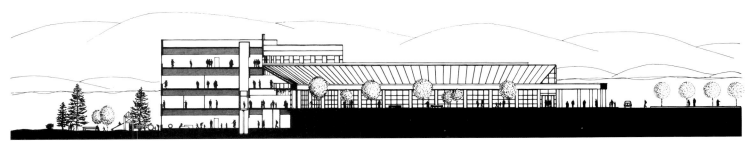

2

To blend the building with its natural surroundings, Fentress Bradburn applied a custom gold-buckskin brick to the building's exterior and interior atrium corridor to reiterate the golden wheat, burnt sage and dramatic mineral soil colorations found in the area. Together with other elements, this enables the building's colors and textures to blend perfectly with the Colorado landscape.

The Jefferson County Human Services Building is a prime example of the firm's expertise at creating visual and physical harmony between a structure and its surrounding environment through exceptional design, superb visual aesthetics and high-quality materials and workmanship.

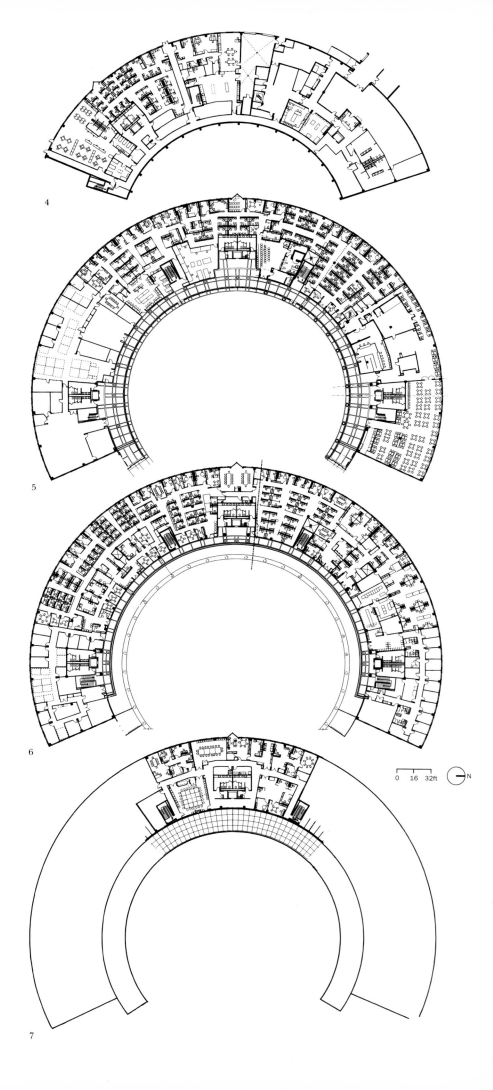

4

5

6

7

3

8

9

10

Ronstadt Transit Center

Design/Completion 1986/1991
Tucson, Arizona
City of Tucson
95,832 square feet
Masonry, light steel frame
Brick, painted steel, concrete block, tiles

Human in scale and feel, Tucson's Ronstadt Transit Center is functional architecture that comfortably accommodates travelers. It also dispels contemporary stereotypes of the urban bus terminal.

Built on a two-block, 2.2-acre site in the historic arts district of Tucson, the transit center is the hub of the local bus system. An arbor runs along two sides of the bus depot, blending the site into its downtown surroundings and providing seats for the convenience of passengers. The entrance archways are faced with recycled turn-of-the-century brick salvaged from local buildings. Tucson artisans crafted the 20,000 ceramic tiles covering the arbor's interior columns and beams.

On the interior, the center is equipped with a variety of sun shelters, shaded areas and landscaping to provide protection from the desert heat. Two cooling towers, modeled on centuries-old wind towers in the Middle East, use technology

Continued

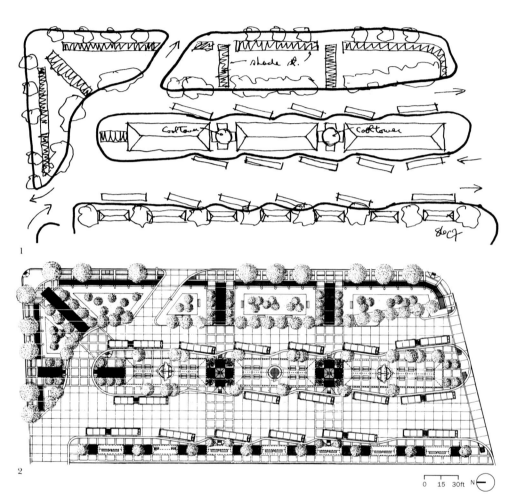

1

2

0 15 30ft N

1 Concept sketch
2 Plaza plan
3 Corner entry gateway
4 Shade canopy

3

4

5

developed at the University of Arizona Environmental Research Laboratory. They water-cool the hot, dry air, reducing the temperature by 10 to 15 degrees within a 20-foot radius of each tower.

As a hub of one of the nation's busiest transport systems, the Ronstadt Transit Center could easily have been one of the dreariest landmarks in downtown Tucson. Instead, it has developed into one of the most likable, humanly scaled, user-friendly projects of its kind, perfectly blended into the surrounding cityscape. Its ingenious design and use of local materials have transformed it into a multi-purpose park and arts facility accommodating a range of events, such as the twice monthly "Downtown Saturday Night Show."

6

7

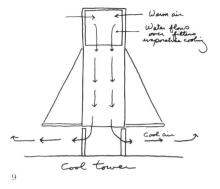

Warm air

Water flows
over filters
evaporative cooling

Cool air

Cool tower

5   Tile detail
6   Shade canopy and seating
7   Sectional elevation
8   Detail of canopy and tower
9   Cool tower concept sketch
10 Shade canopy and seating

8

9

10

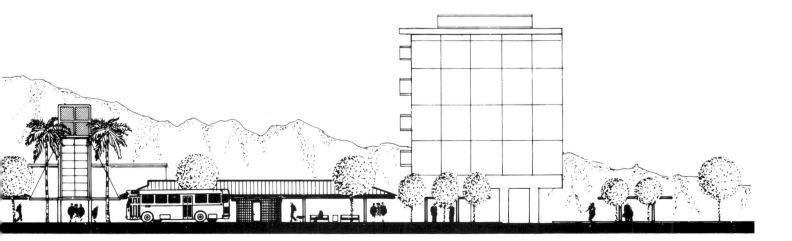

Colorado Convention Center

Design/Completion 1987/1990
Denver, Colorado
City and County of Denver
1,000,000 square feet
Steel frame, precast concrete, long-span steel trusses
Architectural precast concrete, concrete masonry units, glass, terrazzo, gypsum, carpet

The Colorado Convention Center was designed to provide a visionary landmark for the United States convention, exhibition, and meeting industry at a time of great economic development and opportunity.

Fentress Bradburn designed each side of the center to fit into the surrounding urban context. The facade of the exhibition hall is clad in architectural concrete aggregate spandrels, linking its three main entrances with a strong horizontal line. Contrasting vertical and horizontal elements animate the building, whose anchoring weight is lifted by the vertical, wing-like, mechanical penthouses projecting above the cornice line.

As visitors approach from the east, they are welcomed into the building by a concave facade symbolizing outstretched arms. The western facade is curved in the opposite direction to guide visitors' attention towards the panorama of the Rocky Mountains. The southern facade is completed with an upwardly exploding structure of white columns, symbolic of the snow-capped peaks of the Rocky Mountains as they rise above the plains.

Continued

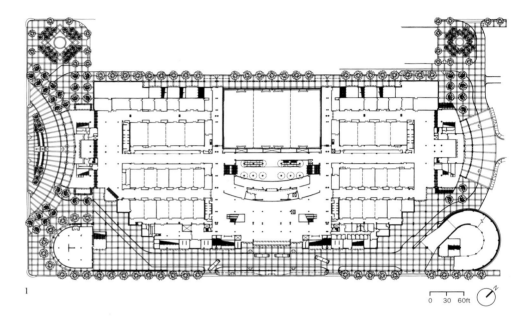

1

0   30   60ft

2

66

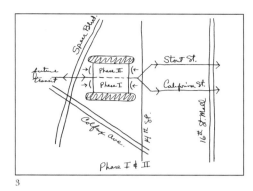

1 Site plan
2 Aerial view
3 Concept sketch
4 Night rendering of entrance
5 Night rendering
6 Exterior at night

3

4

5

6

7

The relationship between the building's forms and geometry is established by a unifying theme throughout the interior. The building contains four activity zones: 65,000 square feet of registration space; 100,000 square feet of meeting space; 300,000 square feet of exhibition space; and a loading dock with 27 bays. These grand spaces make up a "festive, friendly and exciting" project, according to the Urban Land Institute—the nation's most highly respected and widely quoted source of information on urban issues.

This design provides a functional yet dramatic stage for convention activities, in perfect harmony with the facility's exterior. The contemporary materials and colors of the strong horizontal bands on the interior walls mirror those on the exterior and provide an atmosphere of excitement and festivity. The simple but bold geometric forms are a fitting backdrop for convention activities, providing visual continuity throughout the entire complex. The building's simple and distinctive vision of the future provides the city of Denver with an easily identifiable landmark and a positive new image.

8

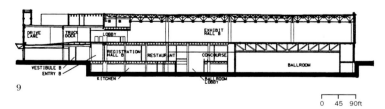

9

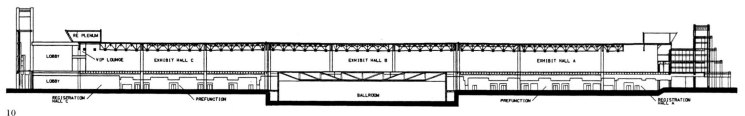

10

12 Welton Street elevation
13 Exterior facade
14 Exhibition hall plan
15 Meeting room plan

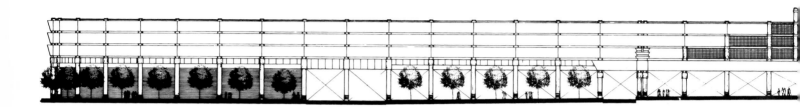

12

13

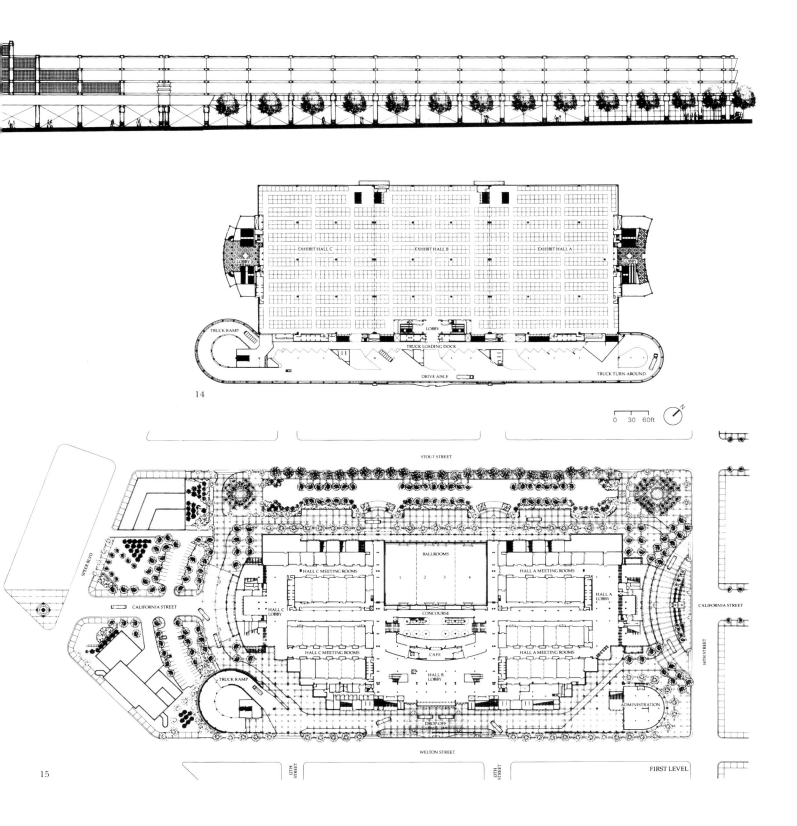

EXHIBIT HALL C   EXHIBIT HALL B   EXHIBIT HALL A

LOBBY

LOBBY

TRUCK RAMP

LOBBY

TRUCK LOADING DOCK

DRIVE AISLE

TRUCK TURN-AROUND

14

0   30   60ft

STOUT STREET

SPEER BLVD

CALIFORNIA STREET

TRUCK RAMP

HALL C MEETING ROOMS

HALL C LOBBY

HALL C MEETING ROOMS

BALLROOMS

1   2   3   4

CONCOURSE

CAFE

HALL B LOBBY

DROP-OFF

HALL A MEETING ROOMS

HALL A LOBBY

HALL A MEETING ROOMS

ADMINISTRATION

CALIFORNIA STREET

14TH STREET

WELTON STREET

12TH STREET

13TH STREET

FIRST LEVEL

15

16   Lobby interior
17   Cafeteria
18   Exhibition hall

16

17

18

Jefferson County Government Center Courts and Administration Building

Design/Completion 1988/1993
Golden, Colorado
Jefferson County Colorado
531,000 square feet
Composite steel frame, concrete core
Architectural precast concrete, glass, sandstone, gypsum, cherry carpet

The Jefferson County Government Center Courts and Administration Building brings together the administrative, law enforcement and judicial functions that were previously dispersed throughout the county. Fentress Bradburn designed this new government center to be surrounded by open space and to offer commanding views across the 93-acre campus. Jefferson County is a mostly rural locality that prides itself on its parks and recreational opportunities. Considerable effort was made to create a landmark that was sensitive to the environment and user-efficient, yet at the same time evoked the reassuring permanence of government.

The structure is divided into two curved wings joined by a central atrium. The wings are designed to reach out into the landscape and physically embody the county's commitment to "serving the people." The central glass rotunda is a nexus for the different branches of government and provides an aesthetic focal point for the building with its lantern-like mass.

Continued

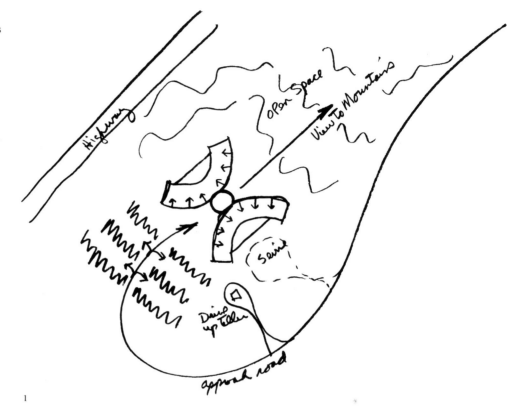

1

1 Concept sketch
2 Exterior view at twilight
3 Entry atrium

2

3

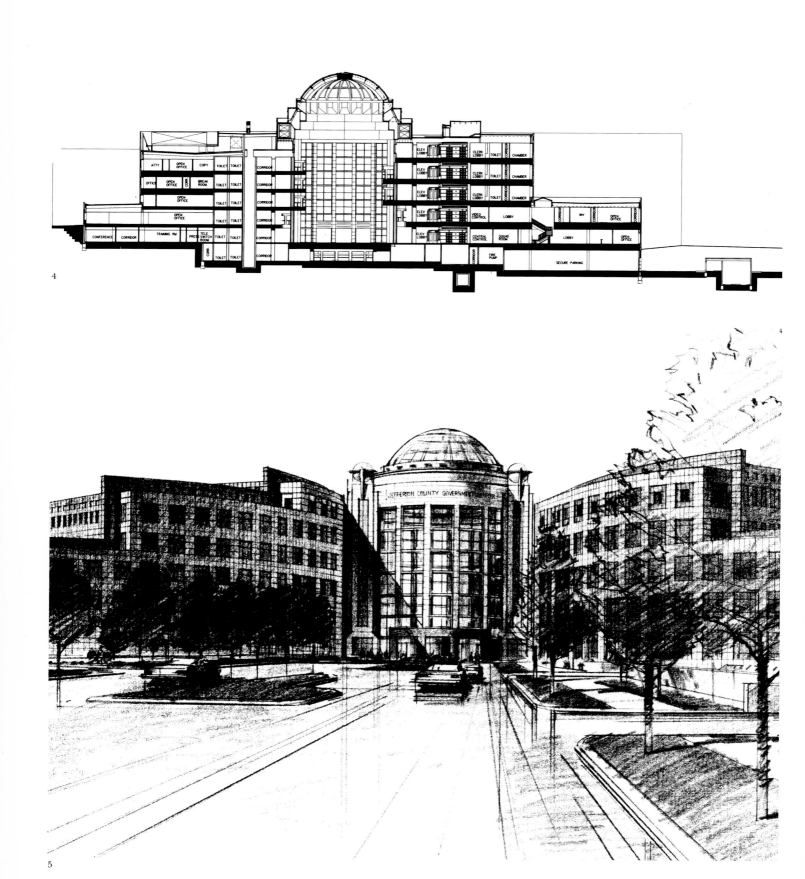

4

5

6

7

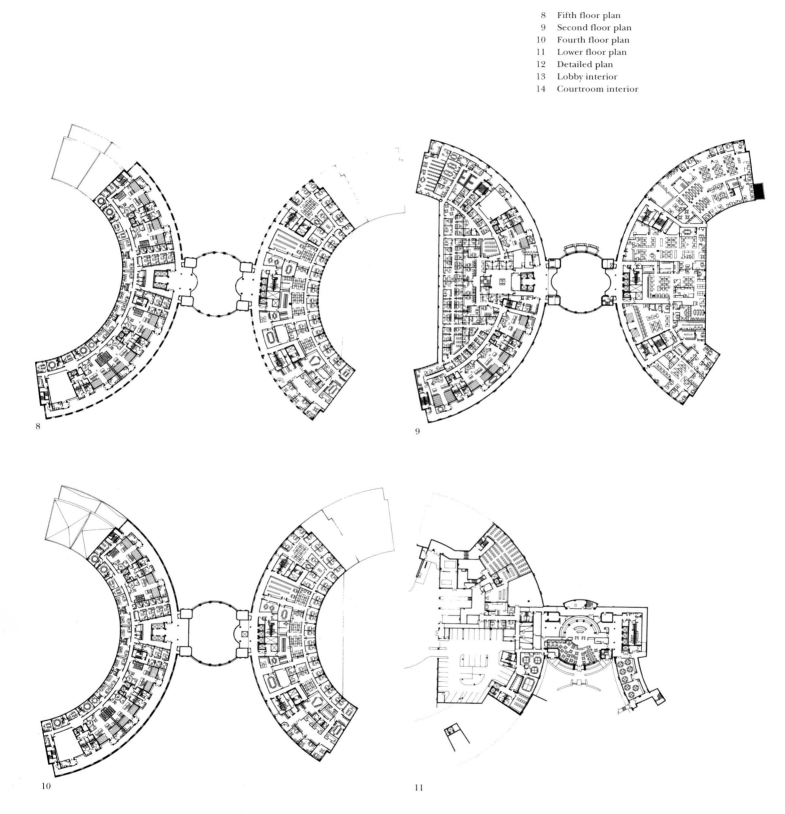

8   Fifth floor plan
9   Second floor plan
10   Fourth floor plan
11   Lower floor plan
12   Detailed plan
13   Lobby interior
14   Courtroom interior

8

9

10

11

Inside, the public corridors follow the building's windowed perimeter and permit majestic views of the Rocky Mountain landscape and the distant city of Denver. Other important features include state-of-the-art energy management and audio-visual security systems as well as a drive-up window facility for express payments.

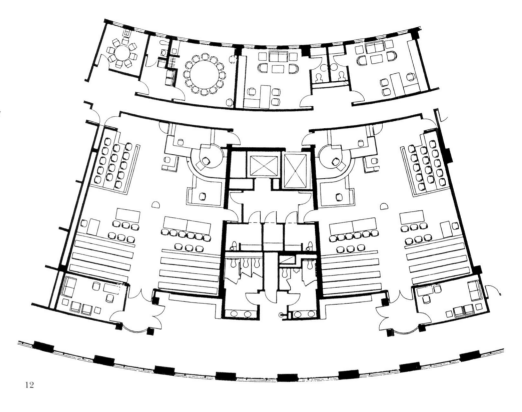

12

13

14

Below:
    Lobby interior dome
Opposite:
    Lobby interior
Following page:
    Lobby interior dome

University of Colorado Mathematics Building and Gemmill Engineering Sciences Library

Design/Completion 1989/1992
Boulder, Colorado
University of Colorado
54,500 square feet
Steel frame, precast concrete
Architectural precast concrete, sandstone, gypsum, carpet

The existence of two master plans for the University of Colorado at Boulder, one by Charles Klauder (1917) and the other by Hideo Sasaki (1960), required the firm to reconsider the meaning of "Colorado architecture."

Blending Sasaki's Modernism with Klauder's revivalist, rural Italian Tuscan style was an architectural challenge in forms and materials. The value of university icons also had to be considered. Native sandstone exteriors and clay tile roofs are used in conjunction with precast concrete to suggest this new Post-Modern ideal. An 80-foot campanile and low-running loggias were planned and direct physical connection was made to the campus network of open greens, quadrangles and strong axial pathways.

Programmed elements include the library, located below grade, and new offices and a faculty commons room above grade. These components are connected to a 400-seat auditorium and the four-story campanile.

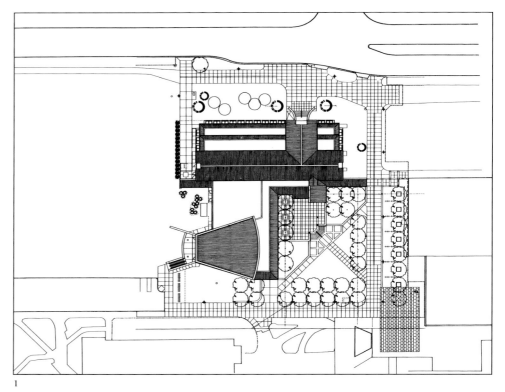

1

2

84

1   Site plan
2&3   Student plaza
4   Campus context
5   Exterior loggia

3

4

5

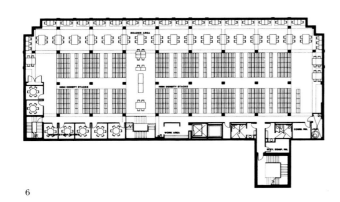

6

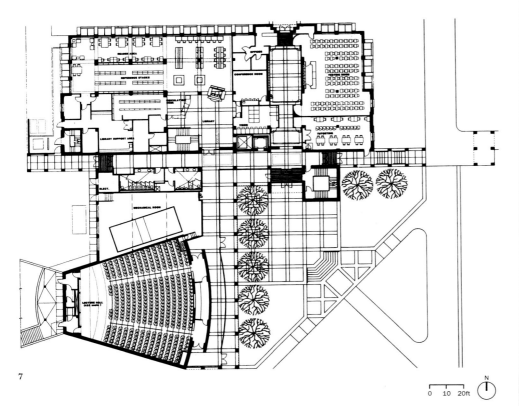

7

0 10 20ft   N

8

9

6   Basement level floor plan
7   Ground level floor plan
8   Auditorium
9   Plaza exterior
10 Second level plan
11 Third level plan

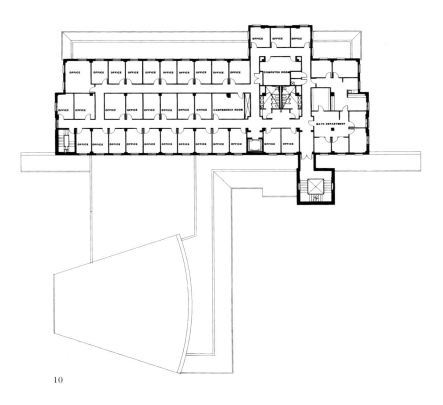

10

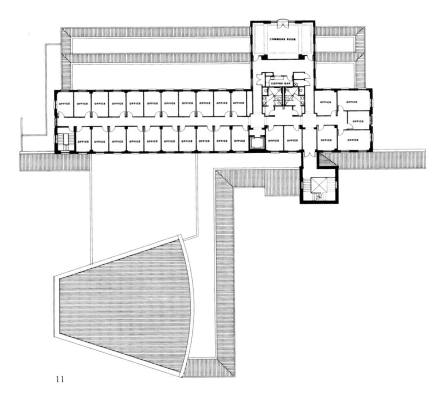

11

Natural Resources Laboratory and Administration Building

Design/Completion 1989/1992
Olympia, Washington
State of Washington, General Services Administration
325,000 square feet
Composite steel frame and concrete core (offices); precast concrete (parking structure)
Acid-etched precast concrete, stucco, limestone, stone, terrazzo, wood

The Natural Resources Laboratory and Administration Building is located on the east campus of the State Capitol complex of Olympia, Washington. It is designed to enhance the original master plan of the west campus by visually tying the two together in both plan and elevation.

The focal point of the building is a rotunda, offset from the main body of the building, but centered on the campus grid. This towered atrium frames and terminates the east campus axis, directly referring to the Capitol as the terminus of the opposite axis.

The building entry through the atrium presents visitors with a lofty centering space. The dramatic, 675-foot curved facade is derived from the geometry of the central campus plan that emanates from the Capitol. The form is comprehensive: it acts as a terminus for the north side of

Continued

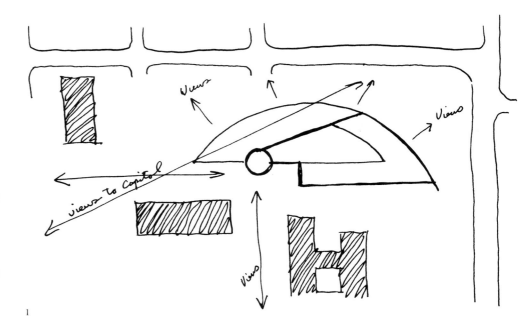

1

2

1   Contextual sketch
2   Exterior at sunset
3   Lower level entrance
4   Laboratory projection
5   "Tree" columns

3

4

5

campus, anchors the east campus and
recalls the rhythm and texture of the
traditional structures of the west campus.
The plan and the design for the building
also incorporate a number of pedestrian
connections to help link east and west.

The landscaping deliberately recreates the
richness of Washington's ecology,
including its forests and wetlands, by
depicting patterns of beach, cobbled
shore, marsh, grassland and forest fringe.
The green trusswork, supported on long
slender columns, evokes a temperate
rainforest canopy, while its cantilever
forms a sunscreen that minimizes solar
impact. Inside, the rotunda's hardwood
columns also allude to a forest
environment, and its terrazzo floor pattern
depicts the winding Columbia River and
the farmlands and forests of eastern
Washington.

Continued

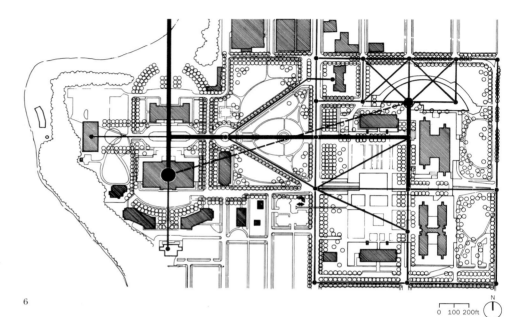

6

0 100 200ft

7

8

The State of Washington, whose departments of fisheries, agriculture, and natural resources are all housed inside the complex, requested a design that would maximize energy conservation and address environmental concerns such as indoor air quality. Fentress Bradburn provided special insulation to minimize air and noise pollution from the high-impact rock-crushing laboratories. Biological and chemical laboratories were located on the top floor. Eco-efficiency is also a key to the interior design, providing occupants with a healthy, open-plan office environment that allows natural daylight to penetrate into even the deepest recesses of the building.

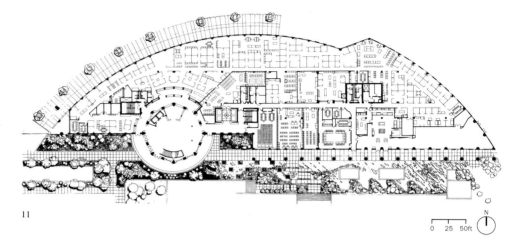

11

0   25   50ft

N

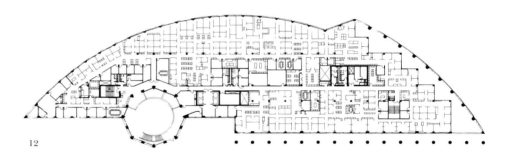

12

10

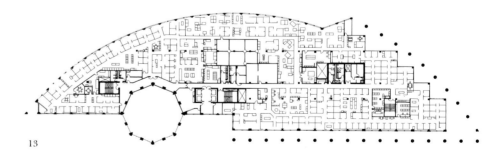

13

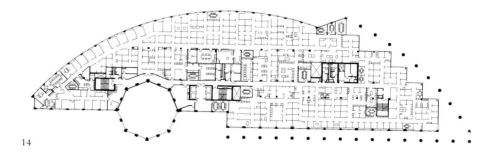

14

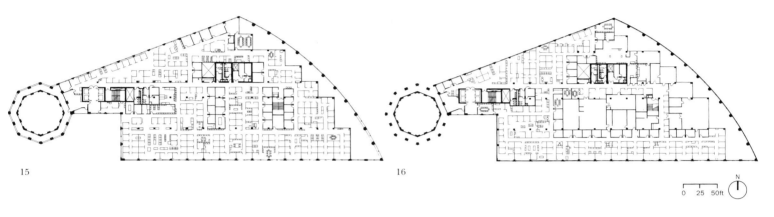

15

16

0 25 50ft   N

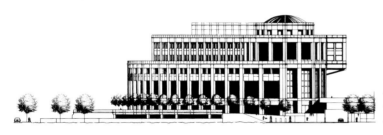

17

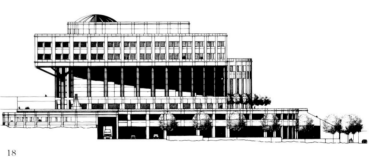

18

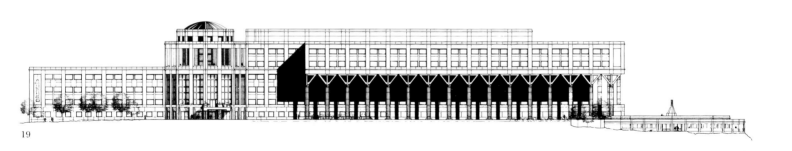

19

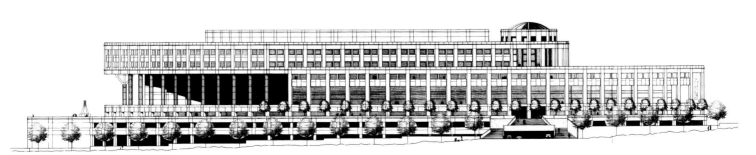

20

21

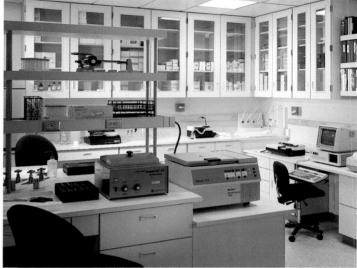

22

23

24

21   Elevator lobby
22   Laboratory
23   Laboratory study area
24   View across atrium
Opposite:
      Lobby interior

IBM Customer Service Center

Design/Completion 1990/1992
Denver, Colorado
IBM
100,000 square feet
Fabric, gypsum, carpet

IBM required a spatially functional interior office design that was sensitive to its image. Fentress Bradburn's IBM Customer Service Center consists of satellite-linked classrooms for participatory classes, a Guided Learning Center where new technology can be explored on IBM equipment, workrooms, conference rooms, faculty meeting rooms, break-out rooms, computer rooms and staff and management offices. The design of this space uses color in a sophisticated manner to reflect IBM's conservative, high-tech image.

A perimeter corridor system, formed by an exterior grid of deep window wells, was specially designed to create the darkened presentation rooms. A wooden grid was designed for the inside wall of the corridor, using beams to tie the two grids together defining each entry. At major intersections, this wooden grid separates into openings designed to define and expand attached reception, waiting and break-out areas. The interior grid is also recessed at the columns to provide special niches for the display of IBM products.

The interior design is an inward extension of the building's exterior facade, carefully exploiting color to communicate the client's image. Thus, the interior walls repeat the curves and beams of the exterior grid to create a sophisticated space that reflects the building's architecture while projecting a unique business identity.

1

2

1 Reception
2 Lecture room
3 Cafeteria
4 Circulation corridor
5 Break area
6 Third floor plan
7 Fourth floor plan

3

4

5

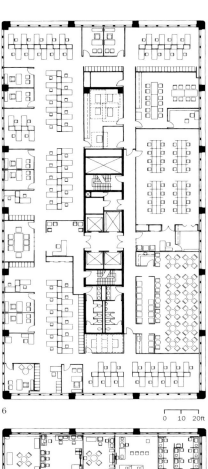

6

0   10   20ft

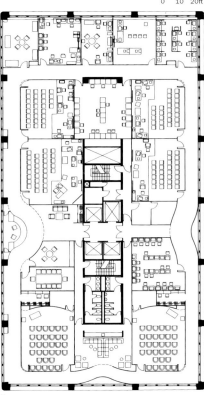

7

Denver International Airport
Passenger Terminal Complex

Design/Completion 1991/1994
Denver, Colorado
City and County of Denver
2,250,000 square feet
Composite steel frame, precast concrete, tensile membrane structure
Architectural precast concrete, Teflon-coated fiberglass, glass, granite, stainless steel

In designing Denver International Airport's Passenger Terminal Complex, Fentress Bradburn created an iconographic symbol for the city of Denver, a memorable showcase of local pride and sense of place. Thus, among other evocations, the terminal building's roof of white peaks—the largest fully enclosed, integrated tensile fabric structure in the world—pays visual homage to the majestic Rocky Mountains. Its undulating fabric of 34 peaks, each rising to a height of 120 feet, encloses the Great Hall, whose design is repeated in the curbside canopies of the drop-off and pick-up areas. The towering, translucent peaks of the Teflon-coated fiberglass roof and the huge expanse of the Great Hall also conjure up the grandeur of the great railway stations of the past, reviving the sense of awe and romance once associated with travel.

Continued

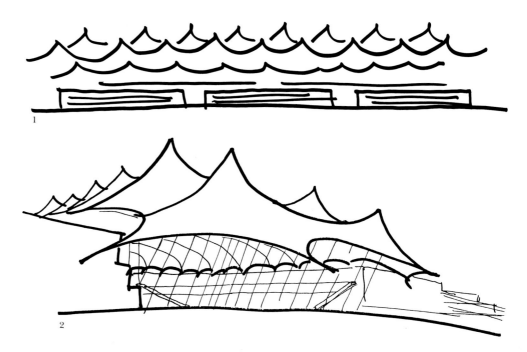

1

2

3

1   Concept sketch
2   South wall sketch
3   Aerial view
4   View from roadside
5   Night view showing roof structure

4

5

6

0 32 64ft

The roof serves a variety of functional and aesthetic purposes. Its curves endow the interior with a very special character, while at the same time it floods the terminal with natural light. This fusion of direct and diffused sunlight brings the indoor and outdoor environments into a kind of symbiosis. In the evening, interior lighting in the Great Hall illuminates the roof fabric, making the peaks luminous and visible for miles. On a practical level, the intricately articulated waterproof building skin allows savings on both lighting and cooling costs by reducing energy requirements.

The entire passenger terminal complex is designed using state-of-the-art building materials to create a user-friendly facility with high levels of comfort, convenience and efficiency.

This gateway to Denver is a unique place that has already begun to leave a lasting mark on international airport design.

7

8

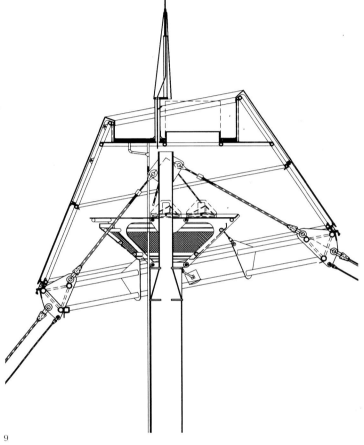

9

10

11

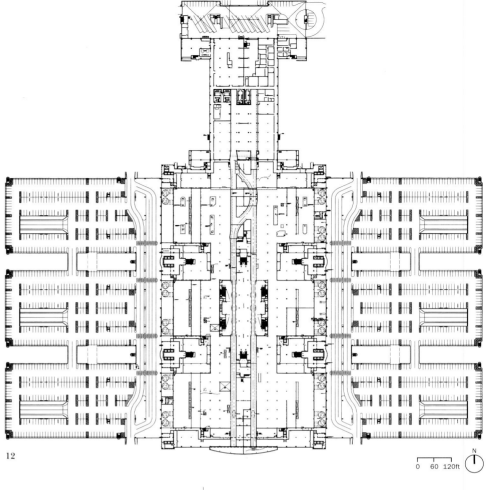

12

0 60 120ft   N

13

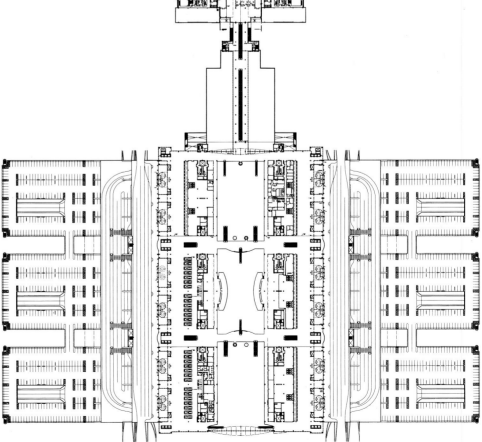

14

15

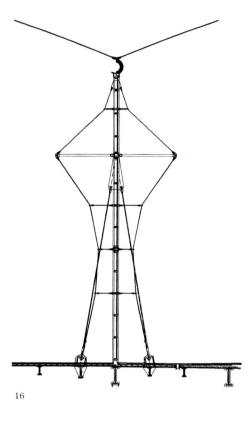

16

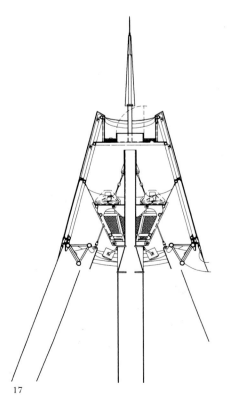

17

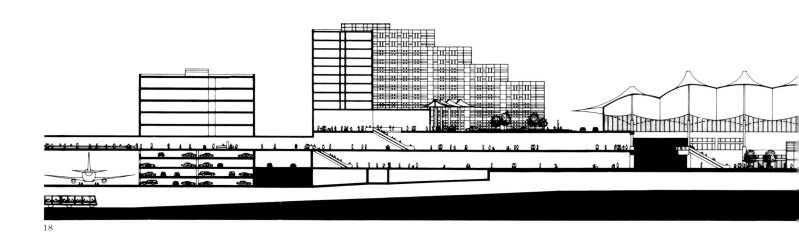

18

19

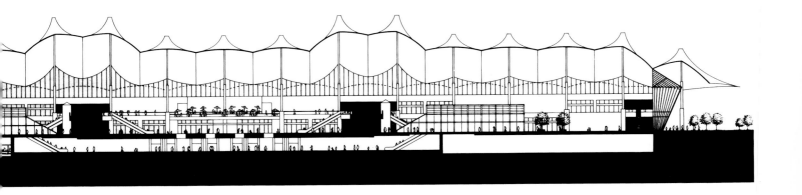

20

22

23

24

25

26 Lights and columns
27 People-mover platform
Opposite:
    Great Hall interior

26

27

National Museum of Wildlife Art

Design/Completion 1991/1995
Jackson, Wyoming
National Museum of Wildlife Art
55,453 square feet
Steel frame, concrete
Stone, glass, wood, gypsum, carpet

The design for the National Museum of Wildlife Art is the embodiment of Fentress Bradburn's theoretical explorations of contextual regionalism. The physical and visual impact of the Grand Tetons has been maximized through the creation of an ecologically sensitive and human-scale building that embraces its site while setting new standards in architectural design.

Since no conventional architectural design was deemed appropriate to this site, Fentress Bradburn created something entirely new. The rough stone cladding and irregular plan of this "building-as-landscape" allow it to coexist naturally with the surrounding rock formations. The winding approach to the museum evokes a sense of discovery as visitors traverse the hillside of the butte upon which it sits. In a similar way of unfolding and revealing, the building draws visitors in, allowing them glimpses of the canyon-like lobby with animal tracks etched into the stone floor, then leading them down a grand, cascading staircase and delivering them to the museum floor.

In this multi-use facility, a new paradigm is created for a community in which a native style of architecture has truly sprung from the earth.

1

2

1 View from across elk refuge
2 Concept elevation
3 Museum viewed from below
4 Exterior dining/viewing terrace

3

4

5   View at dawn
6   Exterior against Sleeping Indian Mountain range

6

7 Axonometric of plan
8 Auditorium
9 View of terrace during winter

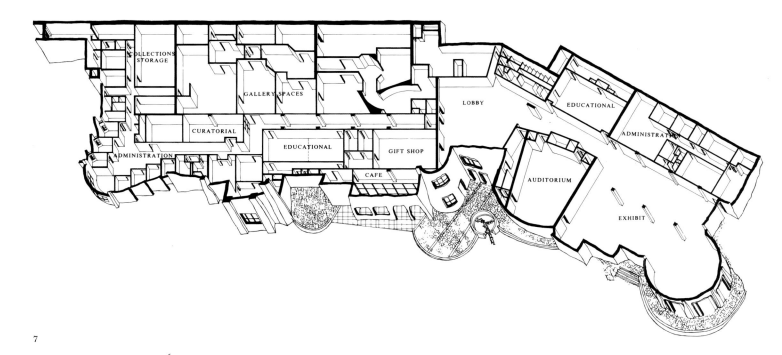

7

8

9

10

10 Winter's night view of entry canopy
11 Two-story lobby space
12 Winter twilight view of entry canopy

11

12

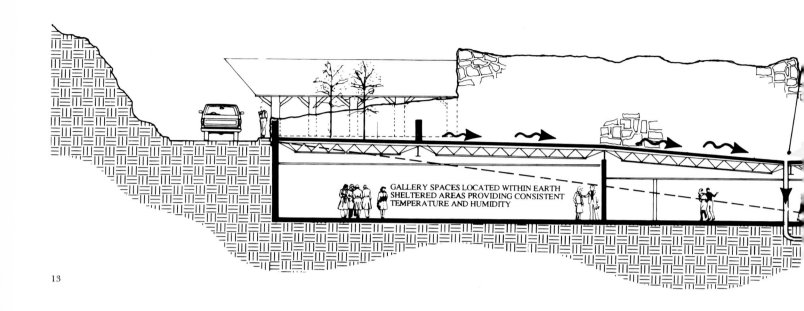

GALLERY SPACES LOCATED WITHIN EARTH
SHELTERED AREAS PROVIDING CONSISTENT
TEMPERATURE AND HUMIDITY

13

14

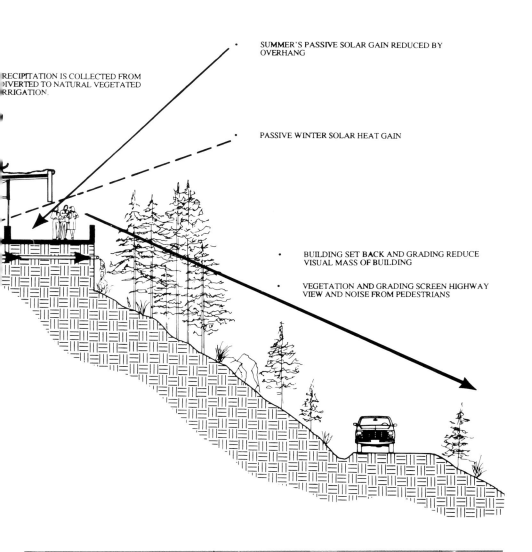

SUMMER'S PASSIVE SOLAR GAIN REDUCED BY OVERHANG

PRECIPITATION IS COLLECTED FROM
DIVERTED TO NATURAL VEGETATED
IRRIGATION.

PASSIVE WINTER SOLAR HEAT GAIN

BUILDING SET BACK AND GRADING REDUCE
VISUAL MASS OF BUILDING

VEGETATION AND GRADING SCREEN HIGHWAY
VIEW AND NOISE FROM PEDESTRIANS

15

13   Section of natural systems
14   Winter view of building and butte
15   Gallery
Following page:
    Entry lobby accessing bookstore, library,
    auditorium and galleries

National Cowboy Hall of Fame

Design/Completion 1991/1997
Oklahoma City, Oklahoma
National Cowboy Hall of Fame
163,000 square feet (expansion); 77,000 square feet (renovation)
Steel frame
Sandstone, stucco, painted metal, fabric, wood, carpet

The creation of a new museum image, a functional, practical building plan and an ideal environment for the display of art, are key to the design of Fentress Bradburn's National Cowboy Hall of Fame. The design concept is a contextual interpretation of the architectural symbols in the original building's design, thus enhancing the profile of the existing museum, while creating a harmoniously sited facility with greater functionality and flexibility.

The comprehensive architectural design draws context and cultural inspiration from Oklahoma City itself, capturing the spirit of the American West. The firm reinterpreted Western images, such as covered wagons and camp tents, in the outstretched canopy that draws visitors to the entrance of the Hall of Fame. The interiors then open into large and brightly lit exhibition spaces that guide visitors through the displays.

Italian architectural critic Maurizio Vitta wrote that, "the architects have succeeded in creating an 'international' icon of the American frontier and, by extrapolation, of America herself."

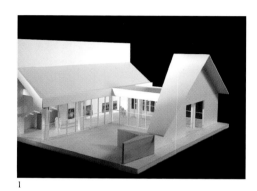

1

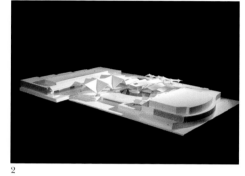

2

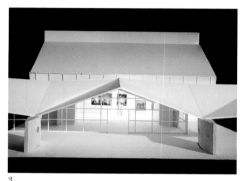

3

4

5

122

6

7

8

10

11

12

13

14

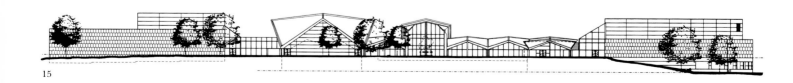

15

16

17

18

19

20

21

22

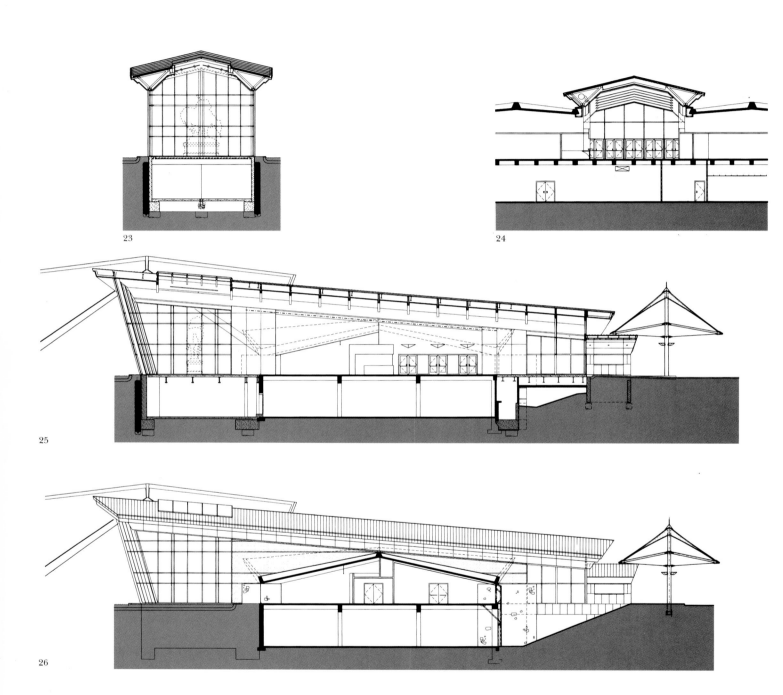

23

24

25

26

27

28

28   Interior of large convention hall
Opposite:
      Hall adjacent to Gaylord wing

Clark County Government Center

Design/Completion 1992/1995
Las Vegas, Nevada
Clark County General Services Department
350,000 square feet
Composite steel frame, concrete core
Sandstone, glass, painted metal, granite, bronze, wood

Inspired by the desert environment of Clark County, Nevada, Fentress Bradburn's Clark County Government Center mirrors the areas natural and man-made ecology. It is a distinctive architectural statement reflecting the varied contemporary trends and historical aspects of the region that is home to Las Vegas.

The plan of the complex is developed around an exterior public space that recalls the historical county courtyard. In this oasis-like setting, a distinctive outdoor stage provides a focal point for performances and public addresses. The architectural forms and courtyard design are inspired by the surrounding desert ecosystem. Thus, the architecture metaphorically embodies the essence of the region by emphasizing the sculptural qualities of its physical environment. Rose-tinted windows are inserted into the natural sandstone cladding. Inspired by the natural hues and materials of the surrounding landscape, they lend the project a timeless permanence.

Continued

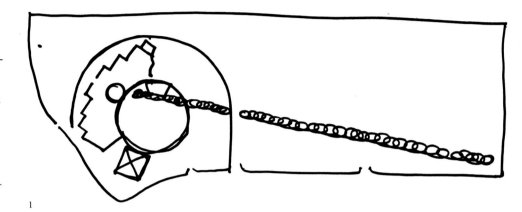

1

2

3

4

5

6

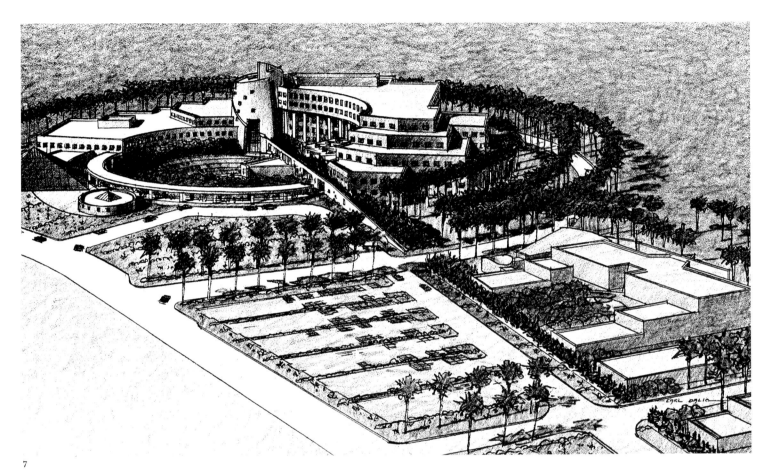

7

8

9

10

The cafeteria is shaped in the form of a pyramid, reflecting the angular rock formations of the desert, while the entry rotunda and County Room lobby visually recall the desert's sculptural rock strata. The commissioners' auditorium chamber is capped by an array of clerestory lights inspired by prickly pear cactus spines. The combined formation blocks out the intense, direct desert sunlight and allows cooler, indirect light to filter through to the interiors.

The campus's overall shape is like a figure from an ancient petroglyph. This image of the area's cultural heritage combined with the outstretched, welcoming arms of the complex, yields an expression of open and accessible government.

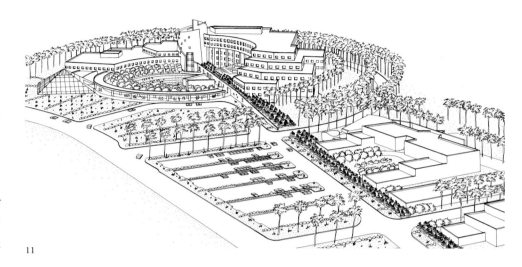

11

12

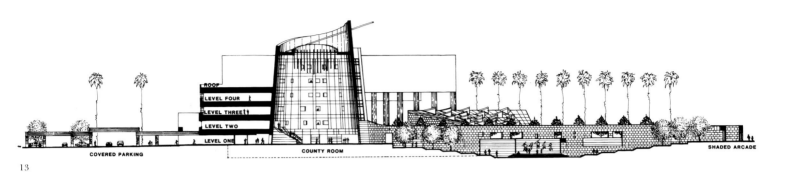

13

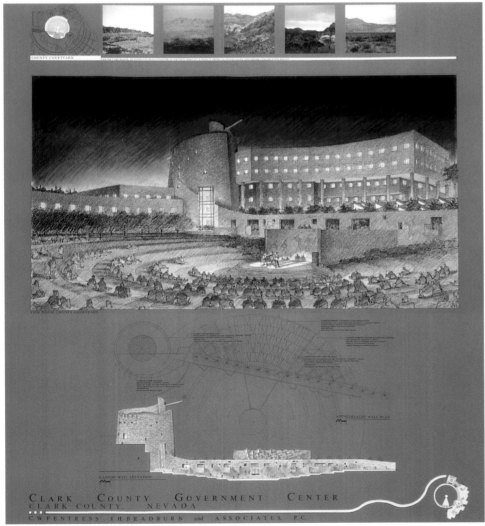

15

16

11 Linear axonometric of the site
12 Presentation board: level one plan
13 Building section through amphitheater
14 Presentation board: view inside county courtyard
15 Cafeteria interior
16 Auditorium/council chambers

14

17 Fourth, fifth and sixth floor plans
18 First, second and third floor plans
19 Model: site overview
20 Model: entry allée

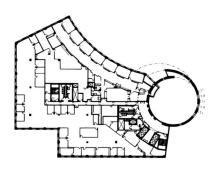

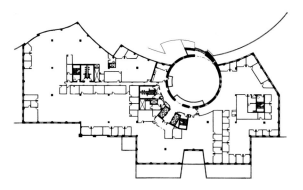

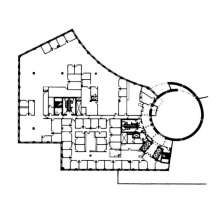

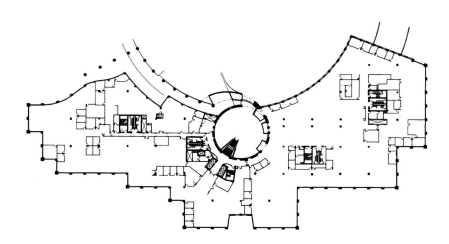

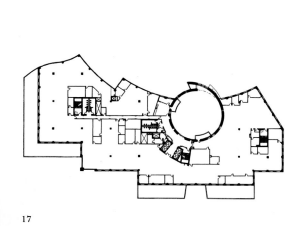

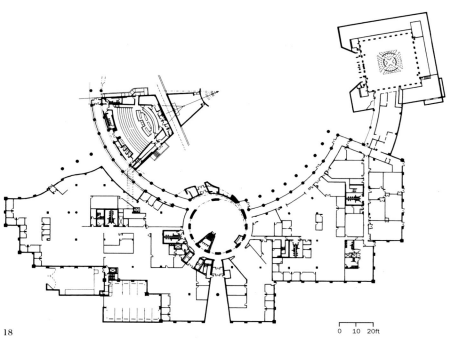

17

18

0   10   20ft

138

19

20

21

22

23

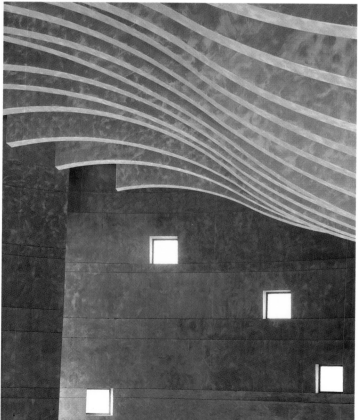

24

27

26 Exterior view
27 Entry lobby with sculptural lights

28

28   Council chamber
Opposite:
   Commissioners' podium

National Oceanic and Atmospheric Administration Boulder Research Laboratories

Design/Completion 1992/1998
Boulder, Colorado
General Services Administration
371,500 square feet
Cast-in-place flat plate concrete
Panelized architectural precast concrete, sandstone, terrazzo

The National Oceanic and Atmospheric Administration's Boulder Research Laboratories are located in the eastern shadow of Boulder's picturesque icon; the Flat Irons geological formation of the Rocky Mountains.

The building is tiered at both ends, resembling the irregular and variegated surfaces of the surrounding foothills. Its elevations are carefully sculpted by a dynamic window pattern set into walls of native flagstone. These materials were chosen for their environmental appropriateness and their compatibility with the larger Colorado context. Building entrances allude to the scientific studies housed within, while the sculpted plaza paving connotes geological erosion. Thus, the multifaceted mass and irregular surface create an intriguing interplay of light and shadow. In a broader context, these rhythms and repetitions of shadow, shade, sunlight and clouds, create a harmony of building and landscape.

The final building design is a striking architectural achievement, compatible with the adjacent research park and residential areas as well as I.M. Pei's National Center for Atmospheric Research which stands above it on the Flat Irons mesa.

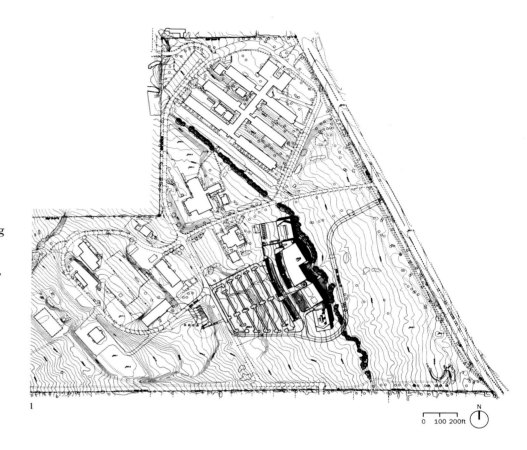

1

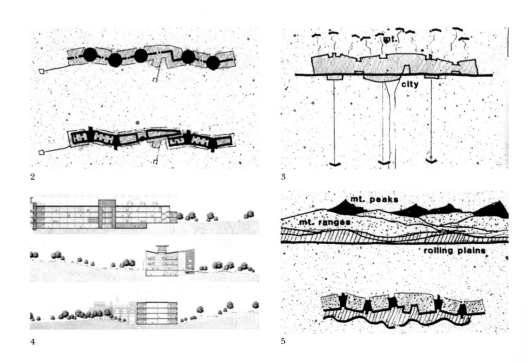

2

3

4

5

146

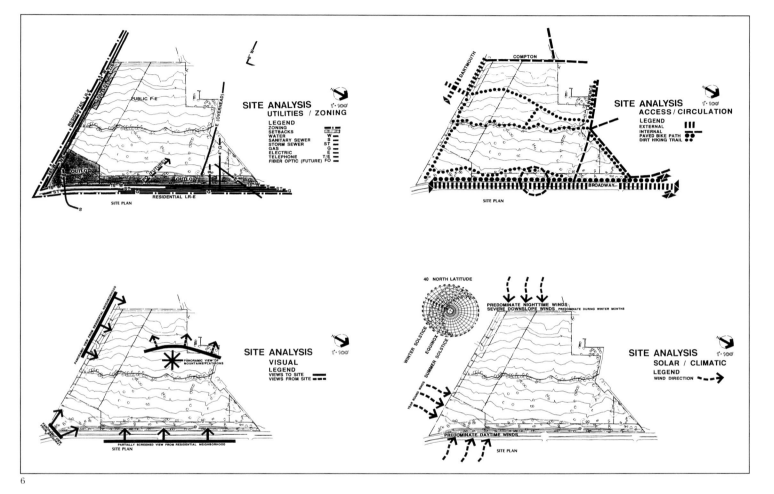

6

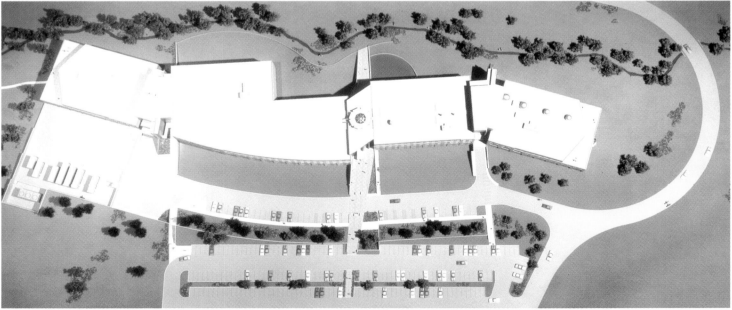

7

8

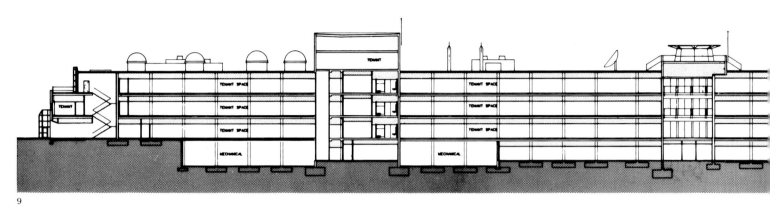

9

10

11

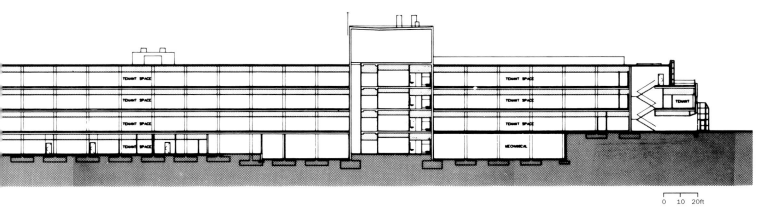

0 10 20ft

12

Second Bangkok International Airport

Design 1993
Bangkok, Thailand
Airport Authority of Thailand
7,000,000 square feet
Steel frame, concrete, long-span steel trusses
Architectural precast concrete, stone, glass, granite, wood, stainless steel

The Second Bangkok International Airport is designed to be rich in symbolic images of the Thai people and their traditions. Fentress Bradburn's design serves not only as a physical, but also as a metaphorical international gateway to Southeast Asia.

In Thai culture, landscape plays an important role. This is evoked by the airport's location amidst lavish garden settings, and through the incorporation of the colors, fragrances and natural beauty of the local vegetation into the building. The runways, taxiways and concourses create a physical progression that mimics the waterways of Bangkok. The passenger terminal is designed as an abstracted lotus flower, the venerated icon of Buddhism seen in much of the nation's architecture. The dynamic form of the terminal roof recalls the upsweeping roof designs of traditional Thai structures. Ocher and green roof tiles emulate the rich soils and lush vegetation of Thailand. Floor designs of granite and carpet follow the iconographic Buddhist patterns of life: wind, water, fire and earth.

This monumental gateway to Bangkok is intended to become a treasured national landmark and a source of pride for the entire nation of Thailand as a universal showcase for its arts, tradition and culture.

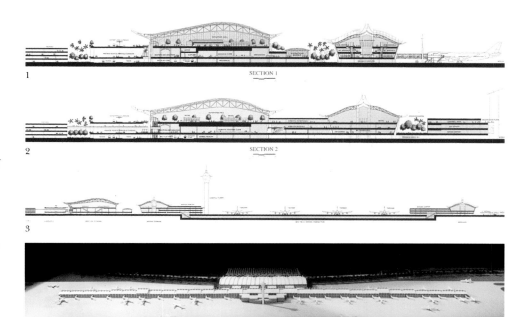

1

SECTION 1

2

SECTION 2

3

4

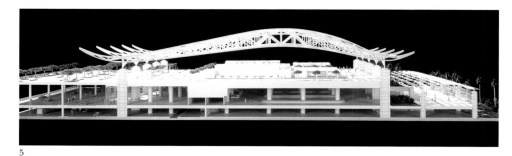

5

6

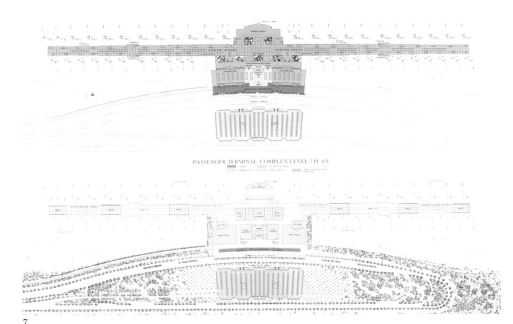

PASSENGER TERMINAL COMPLEX-LEVEL 2 PLAN

7

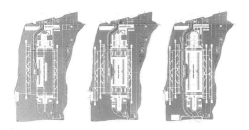

8

9

10

Kwangju Bank Headquarters

Design 1993
Kwangju, Republic of Korea
Kwangju Bank
700,000 square feet
Composite steel frame, concrete core
Stone, glass, gypsum, carpet

The Kwangju Bank Headquarters building creates a new symbol of prosperity, and reflects South Korea's burgeoning economy. It will help transform Kwangju, the historical agricultural center of southeast Korea, into a major center of trade and business.

Fentress Bradburn's design is inspired by its Korean cultural context both in its coloration and patterning. The facade is detailed at its multiple cornice lines to suggest bowed Asian beams. The rhythm of the glass and natural stone course mimics the patterns used in traditional Korean fabric. The mass of the building responds in typically Korean cultural fashion to the dichotomy between the past and the future.

The 35-story Kwangju Bank Headquarters is the first high-rise building in which Fentress Bradburn's contextual regionalism has been fully applied. The resulting design has an indefinable quality that affords viewers the pleasure of an image that is at once strangely familiar and entirely new.

1

1   Concept sketch
2   Rendering of building
3&4   Model
5   Levels 29–47 plan
6   Levels 7–28 plan
7   Level 6 plan
8   Street level plan

2

3

4

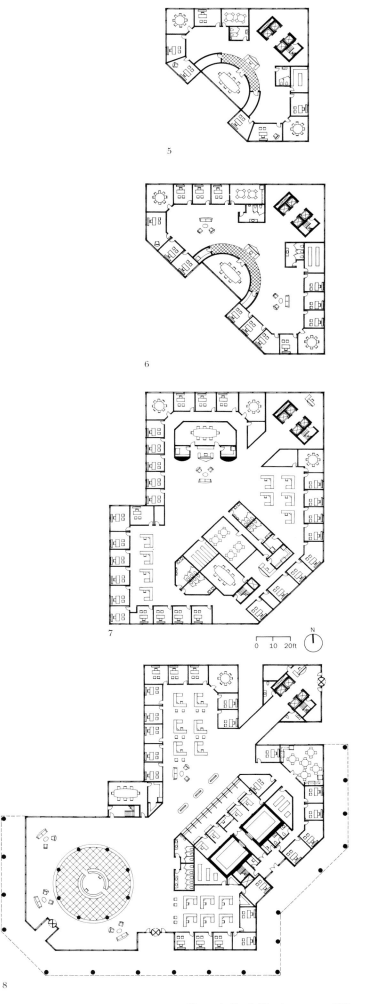

5

6

7

0   10   20ft   N

8

David Eccles Conference Center and Peery's Egyptian Theater

Design/Completion 1993/1996
Ogden, Utah
Weber County Commission, Weber State University
80,000 square feet
Steel frame on existing structural masonry
Brick, terra cotta tiles, limestone, glass

The David Eccles Conference Center and Peery's Egyptian Theater are designed as part of the City of Ogden's downtown revitalization plan. A two-story structure combining local sandstone, precast concrete accent and glass atrium lobby rises on Washington Boulevard. This attaches to a fully restored 1929 Egyptian-style theater, the new home for the Utah Musical Theater Company. The project encompasses 80,000 square feet of conference and meeting room facilities, including a 15,000-square-foot ballroom and 40,000 square feet of performing arts and off-stage support space, as well as the restored 867-seat theater and fly gallery.

Revitalizing Ogden's Egyptian revival-style theater, a former center for the performing arts, involved incorporating significant new elements to generate an architectural identity worthy of its predecessor. What emerged is a multipurpose center for several important cultural arts organizations, including the resident company, Weber State University, meeting planners and the Utah Lodging Association.

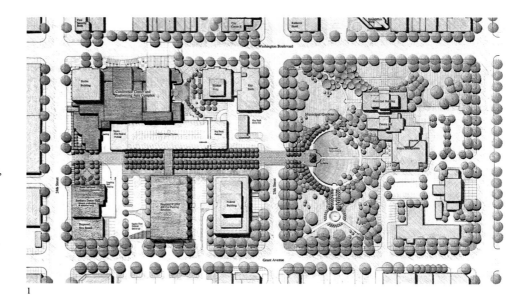

1

2

1 Site plan
2 Early rendering
3 View of Washington Boulevard facade
4 Washington Boulevard elevation
5 Detail of Washington Boulevard facade

3

154

4

0 16 32ft

5

6   Day view of 24th Street
7   Night view of 24th Street facade
8   Night view of Washington Boulevard facade
9   Night view of main entry

6

7

8

9

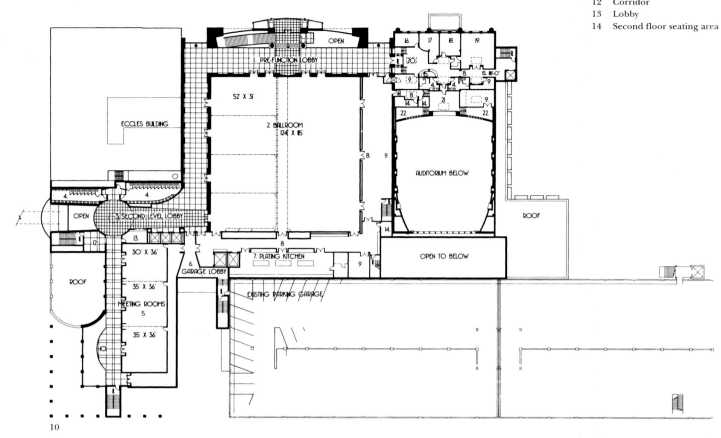

10

0   16   32ft   N

WASHINGTON BOULEVARD

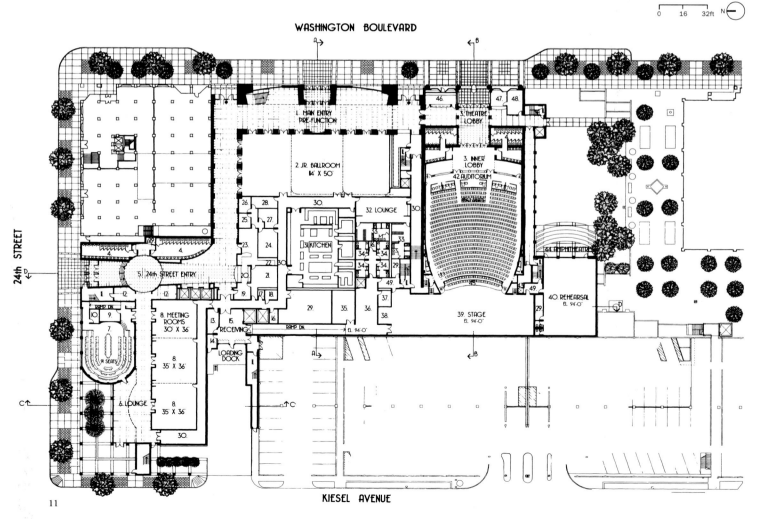

11

12

13

14

15   Egyptian Theater ceiling detail
16   Egyptian Theater lobby
17   Egyptian Theater entrance
18   Egyptian Theater interior

15

16

17

18

Colorado Christian Home Tennyson Center for Children and Families

Design/Completion 1993/1996
Denver, Colorado
National Benevolent Association
63,700 square feet
Light steel frame, reinforced masonry
Brick, painted metal, wood, glass, tiles, wood, gypsum, carpet

Winston Churchill's profound statement, "First we shape our buildings and thereafter they shape us," greatly influenced the design of the new Colorado Christian Home Tennyson Center for Children and Families. Buildings in which we live, play and go to school affect how we feel about ourselves, how we communicate with each other and what image we project as a society. Buildings can also evoke emotion, engraving on our minds lifelong memories of a place. The memories that shape us are most frequently those inspired by the spaces of our childhood. The center, both a school and a home, has the potential to guide and inspire such memories.

Established in 1904 as an orphanage, the center is a non-profit organization which provides residential housing, therapy and education for abused children aged 5–12 as well as therapy for their families.

Although the home was originally planned off site, Fentress Bradburn's master plans generated several options which demonstrated how the requirements for the new design could fit comfortably

Continued

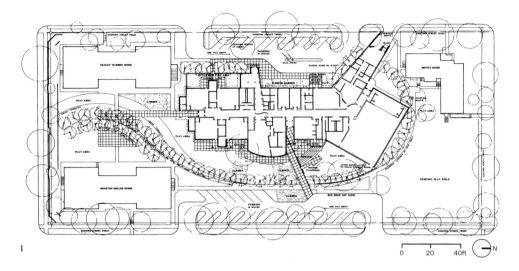

1

2

1   Site plan
2   West view
3&4   East views

3

4

within the existing campus. This enabled the center to realize substantial savings in fulfilling its goal of "unifying the child's experience of living, playing, healing and learning."

All aspects of the design were unified to create a common theme of home, not institution. As a result, many aspects of the landscaping, architecture and interior design are playful and colorful, yet foster images of caring and stability.

The concept of creating a home is also a thoughtful response to the existing residential neighborhood. The exterior design grew from its surroundings, incorporating colors, materials, and building forms which matched its context, maintaining a park-like setting and creating a focus for the community.

5

6

7

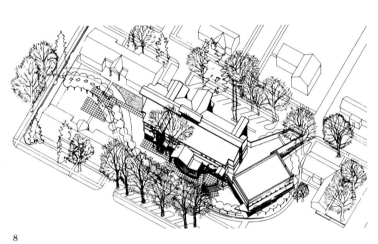

8

9

10

11

12

Montrose County Justice Center

Design/Completion 1993/1998
Montrose, Colorado
Montrose County, Colorado
110,000 square feet
Precast concrete, concrete block, light steel framing
Brick veneer, stone, synthetic stucco, sandstone, wood, carpet

This development incorporates three major elements: a new Colorado Seventh Judicial District courthouse; a Montrose, San Miguel, and Ouray county jail facility; and a sheriff's building. The courts complex includes space for the combined State District Courts and County Courts, a Water Court, the Clerk of the Combined Court, jury assembly, a law library, judicial district administration, probation, district attorney and child support administration. To maintain security and provide the vital segregation of functions, a three-part circulation system is utilized for judges, members of the public and prisoners.

The jail includes state-of-the-art direct-supervision day rooms, a maximum security dorm, a women's dorm and a work-release facility. The jail is designed in two modules to house 192 prisoners. A third module can be added in the future to expand the jail to 264 beds.

The main urban design challenge was to incorporate the facility into a downtown site bordered by residential and light commercial use, and situated along a state highway with its associated "strip" development. The result is a 25-year master plan that provides expansive flexibility.

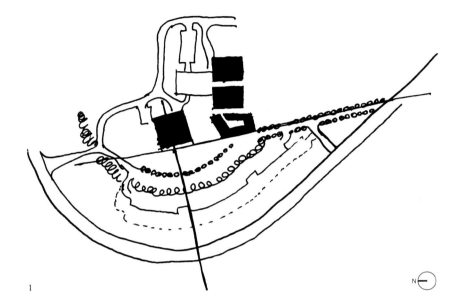

1

2

3

1   Concept sketch
2   Approach elevation
3   Entrance elevation
4   Jail section at dayroom
5   Jail longitudinal section
6   First floor plan

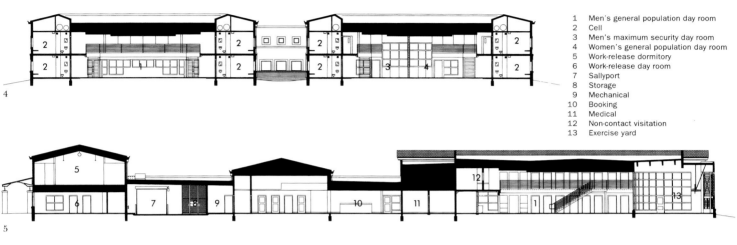

1	Men's general population day room
2	Cell
3	Men's maximum security day room
4	Women's general population day room
5	Work-release dormitory
6	Work-release day room
7	Sallyport
8	Storage
9	Mechanical
10	Booking
11	Medical
12	Non-contact visitation
13	Exercise yard

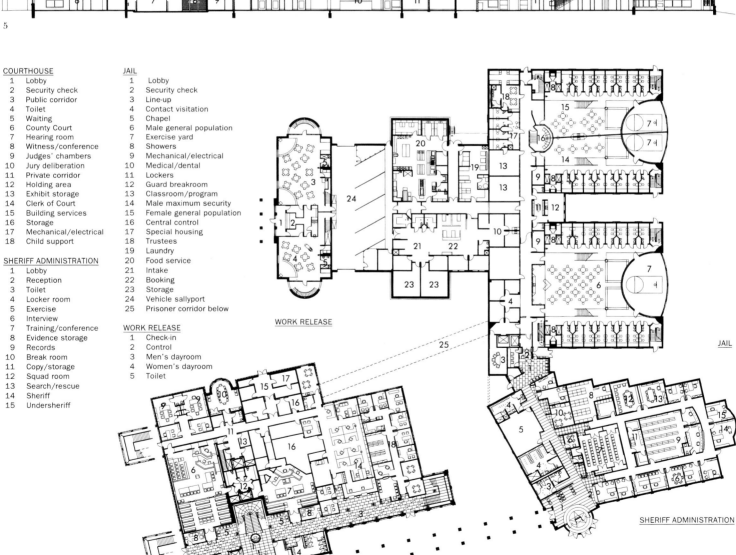

COURTHOUSE
1	Lobby
2	Security check
3	Public corridor
4	Toilet
5	Waiting
6	County Court
7	Hearing room
8	Witness/conference
9	Judges' chambers
10	Jury deliberation
11	Private corridor
12	Holding area
13	Exhibit storage
14	Clerk of Court
15	Building services
16	Storage
17	Mechanical/electrical
18	Child support

SHERIFF ADMINISTRATION
1	Lobby
2	Reception
3	Toilet
4	Locker room
5	Exercise
6	Interview
7	Training/conference
8	Evidence storage
9	Records
10	Break room
11	Copy/storage
12	Squad room
13	Search/rescue
14	Sheriff
15	Undersheriff

JAIL
1	Lobby
2	Security check
3	Line-up
4	Contact visitation
5	Chapel
6	Male general population
7	Exercise yard
8	Showers
9	Mechanical/electrical
10	Medical/dental
11	Lockers
12	Guard breakroom
13	Classroom/program
14	Male maximum security
15	Female general population
16	Central control
17	Special housing
18	Trustees
19	Laundry
20	Food service
21	Intake
22	Booking
23	Storage
24	Vehicle sallyport
25	Prisoner corridor below

WORK RELEASE
1	Check-in
2	Control
3	Men's dayroom
4	Women's dayroom
5	Toilet

WORK RELEASE

JAIL

SHERIFF ADMINISTRATION

COURTHOUSE

0   16   32ft   N

University of Northern Colorado
Gunter Hall Renovation

Design/Completion 1993/1997
Greeley, Colorado
University of Northern Colorado
92,000 square feet
Steel frame on existing masonry structure
Brick, terra cotta, limestone, ornamental plaster, vinyl, gypsum, carpet

A 1927 Neo-Gothic masterpiece by noted Denver architect William Bowman, Gunter Hall is the signature architectural symbol for the University of Northern Colorado. Since its dedication in 1928, it has served as the campus's athletic facility: "a health center in which all students of the institution are taught the fundamentals of healthful living and care of their bodies."

Gunter Hall's dedication to health is given new meaning in the 1990s as a medical education facility for UNC's College of Health and Human Sciences. The vision of the design was to create a healthy and synergistic professional home for the building's academic departments, as well as students and community members. The design program specified an increase in area from 58,000 to 92,000 square feet. This vast increase in area is integrated into the building without affecting the historic character of its interior and exterior.

Continued

1

2

3

1   Entry with tower
2   Detail of tower
3   Rear elevation
4   Detail of entry

4

Additional space is captured within the existing building in several creative ways. A "building within a building" is inserted into the original main gymnasium. This two-story interior addition is designed around a central atrium and provides new classroom, laboratory, and office space. The atrium maintains the light and airy character of the original gymnasium. It is detailed with new materials, but in a style that complements the original structure. An underground mechanical addition provides space for new equipment without affecting either the building's historic character or its usable tenant area.

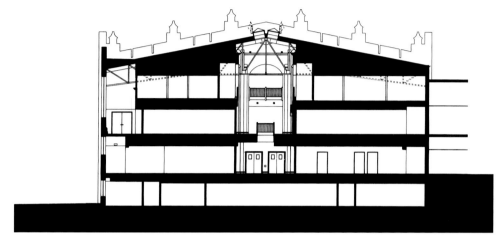

5

0   15   30ft

5   Section
6   Atrium looking up
7   Atrium
8   Classroom
9   Classroom with old windows
10 Third level plan
11 Second level plan
12 First level plan
13 Lower level plan

6

7

8

9

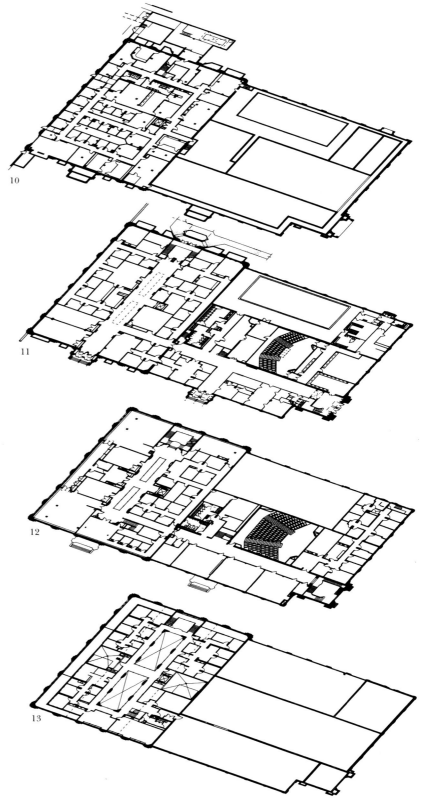

10

11

12

13

One Polo Creek

Design/Completion 1994/1997
Denver, Colorado
BCORP Holdings and AIMCO
203,600 square feet
Cast-in-place concrete with post-tensioned slabs
Brick, limestone, wood, gypsum, tiles, carpet, glass

One Polo Creek represents the union of mid-rise living and single-family residences. The project offers individual identity within a common architectural expression.

Inspired by the grand European home—the Baroque French chateau, Italian villa, English manor house—One Polo Creek reinvents country living in a modern urban setting. The project balances individual privacy with the public amenities of a high-end, multi-family building. Security is emphasized without sacrificing the comfortable transition from private parking to residence. To enhance the country manor image, One Polo Creek is extensively landscaped with formal gardens.

Early chateau and villa massing help maximize views to each point of the compass. Brick masonry reinforces the residential scale, while the stone and

Continued

1

1 Rendering
2 Exterior view
3 Rendered north elevation
4 Entry facade view

2

3

4

concrete articulated base anchors the project in the landscape. Post-tensioned concrete slab construction facilitates the dramatic balcony cantilevers which optimize the unobstructed clear space within individual residences. The 60 residential units and two guest suites have nearly floor-to-ceiling glazing, increasing the natural light within and further enhancing the extraordinary views.

6

5

7

5 Lobby tower
6 Balcony detail
7 Westward view
Opposite:
   Entrance canopy

9

10

11

12

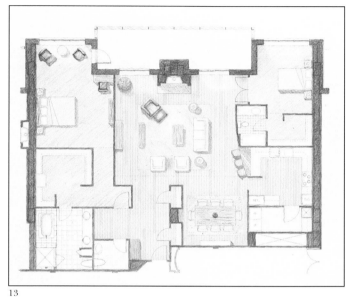

13

14

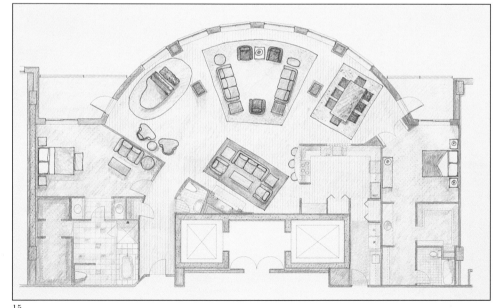

15

9   Bedroom
10   Kitchen
11   Lobby staircase
12   Staircase detail
13   Unit 210 floor plan
14   Fireplace
15   Unit 312 floor plan

New Inchon International Airport Passenger Terminal Complex

Design/Completion 1994/2000
Seoul, Republic of Korea
Korean Airports Authority
5,400,000 square feet
Steel frame, concrete, long-span bow trusses,
cable-stayed steel structures
Architectural precast concrete, metal panels, glass,
granite, wood, stainless steel

Faced with rapidly increasing
transportation demands, the Korean
Ministry of Transportation and Airports
Authority sought to create a new and
memorable gateway to Korea. Built on the
reclaimed land of Young-jong Island in
Inchon Bay, the New Inchon International
Airport is a contemporary architectural
expression wedded to the city's historical
royal past. Ancient and modern culture
merge on the shores of the Yellow Sea.

The airport's design showcases Korean
culture and technology. Its profile is
inspired by historic Korean buildings,
while the shape of the concourse roof
recalls ancient Korean palaces. A wide
range of influences drawn from the
country's ancient culture were translated
into structural forms using local materials,
colors and art forms.

Continued

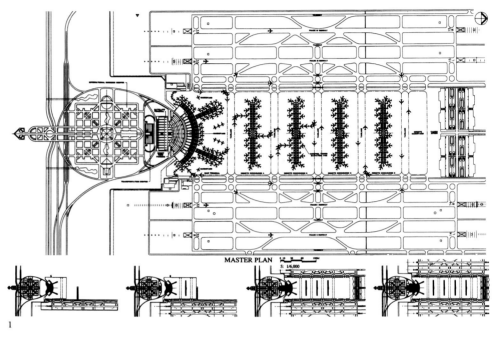

MASTER PLAN

1

2

3

4

5

1 Master plan
2 Model of exterior
3–5 Model of interior
6 Model of terminal

Traffic-flow patterns are established in the Great Hall of the main terminal through which each passenger, visitor and employee must pass. Throughout the facility, natural daylight and interior landscaping create a pleasant ambience. This design also invokes Korea's natural ecological forms, contrasting them with the region's contemporary built environment. Cultural awareness is evident in the Korean-garden-style interior landscaping, the patterning of the floor with images of tiger stripes and the temple detailing of the columns and trusses.

Fentress Bradburn's design establishes the New Inchon International Airport as an international hub and a new gateway to Asia and South Korea. Clearly Korean in inspiration and execution, the airport evokes a lasting and positive image of the country for the travelers passing through its gates.

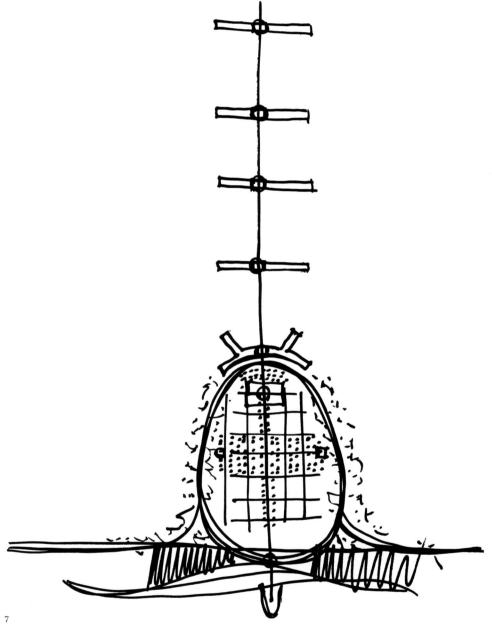

7

8

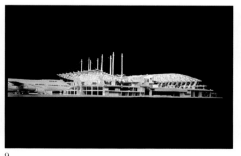

9

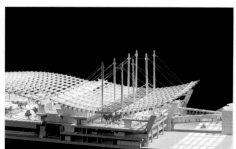

10

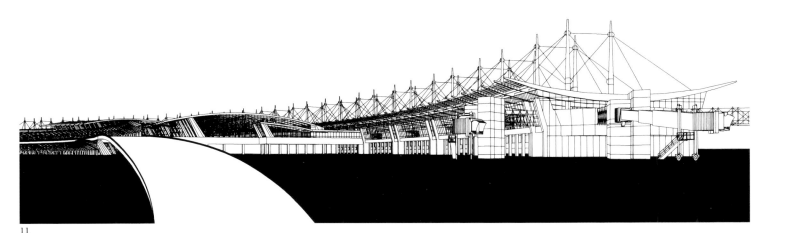

11

12

New Inchon International Airport Passenger Terminal Complex   181

13   Section through terminal and departure concourse
14   Terminal interior
15   Check-in counter
16   Great hall

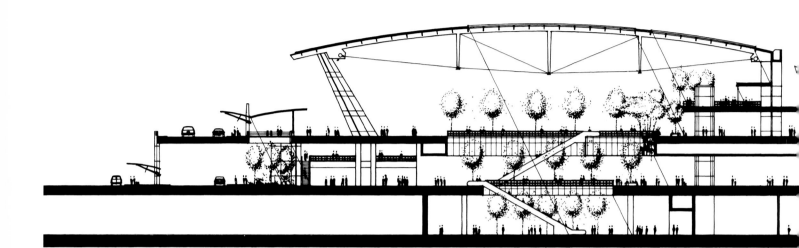

13

14

15

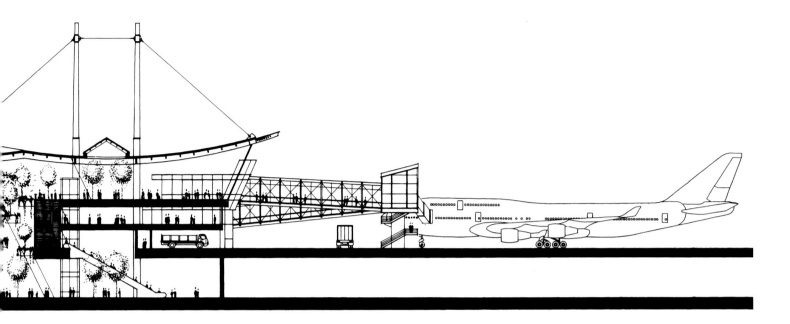

17&18   Model: exterior view at night
19   Terminal check-in
Opposite:
       Passenger drop-off

17

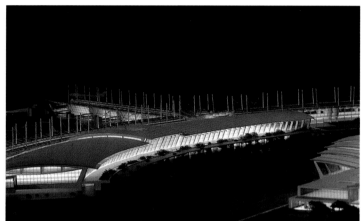

18

19

One Wynkoop Plaza

Design/Completion 1995/1998
Denver, Colorado
Thermo Development Inc.
65,000 square feet
Cast-in-place concrete
Brick, stone, metal, synthetic stucco, tiles, wood,
gypsum, carpet, glass

One Wynkoop Plaza is an exclusive
residential loft development. Owners are
afforded the convenience and amenities
of new construction, while the building
remains compatible with the historic
context of Denver's lower downtown
(LoDo) district adjacent to the city's new
baseball stadium, Coors Field.

Each of the building's 18 units has
separate and direct elevator access that
maintains an exclusive private entry
without the need for a central public
corridor. Each unit also has a balcony with
mountain views to the west and a view of
the city to the east. End units have balcony
views with three different exposures.

The building's brick and stone exterior
cladding and cast-in-place concrete
skeleton frame high-quality residential
materials and integrate the building with
its historical LoDo site. Thus, the exterior
of the building blends with its historical
context while exhibiting an architectural
vocabulary that is a new interpretation of
the local vernacular.

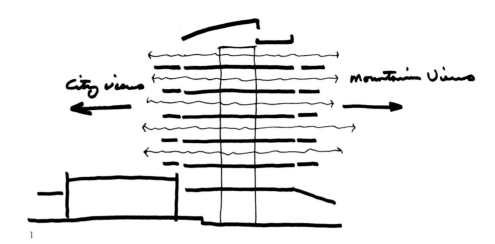

1

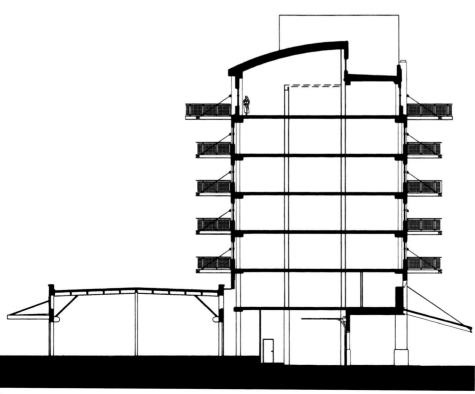

2

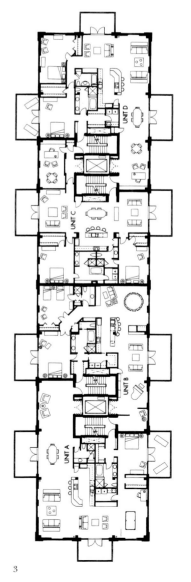

3

1 Concept sketch
2 Section
3 Typical floor plan
4 East elevation
5 Aerial view towards Coors Field
6 Model view
7 Aerial view towards downtown
8 Aerial view towards Elitch Gardens

4

5

6

7

8

City of Oakland Administration Buildings

Design/Completion 1995/1998
Oakland, California
City of Oakland
450,000 square feet (building); 100,000 square feet (parking garage)
Steel, architectural precast concrete, glass
Gypsum, carpet

Historically, the city of Oakland has always labored for recognition in the shadow of its two more prominent neighbors, San Francisco and Berkeley. However, since the 1989 Loma Prieta earthquake, Oakland has invested considerable time and energy in an aggressive campaign to rebuild and repair the city, thereby creating a new sense of permanence and community pride.

Fentress Bradburn's new city administration buildings are added to the old City Hall to fashion a new city government complex. The existing walls and new buildings also demarcate the Frank H. Ogawa Plaza—a *nuevo piazza Americana*. The new buildings' singular attention to detail and articulation are conciously regional, fashioned to fit seamlessly into the local context in both style and scale.

The focus of this new complex is the City Hall Building, designed to complement the old City Hall's historic presence through its scale, massing, color and material. The main entrance to each of the new buildings is expressively articulated and carefully positioned to simplify architectural interrelationships on the plaza.

These new buildings enhance Oakland's urban fabric and create a new and cohesive civic presence by revitalizing the downtown center.

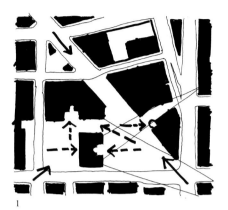
1

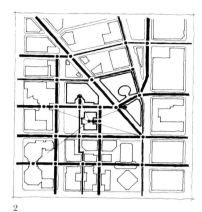
2

3

"ENTRY"

"CORNER BAY"

"BASE · MIDDLE · TOP"

"CORNICE"

4

188

1   City room
2   Linkages
3&4   Rendering of Dalziel block
5   Broadway Building ground floor plan
6   Broadway Building sixth floor plan
7   Broadway Building block
8   Site plan

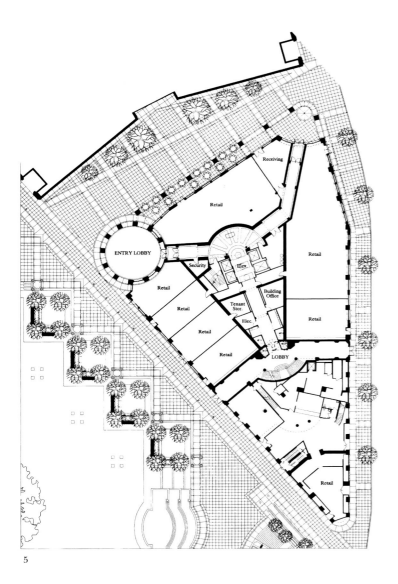

5

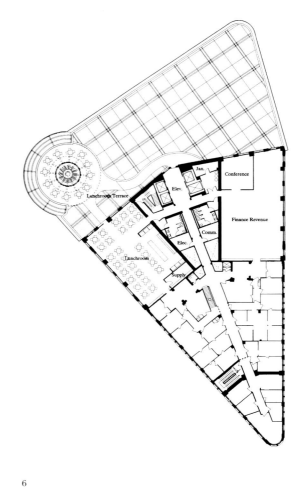

6

7

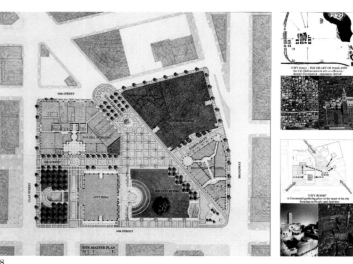

8

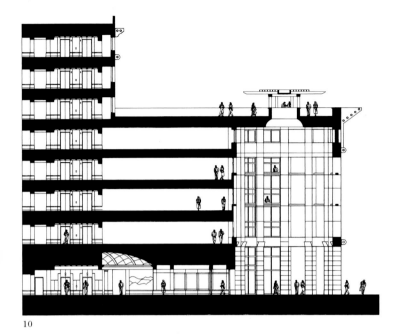

10

13

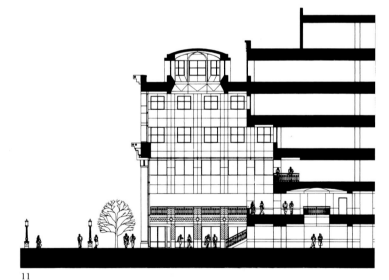

11

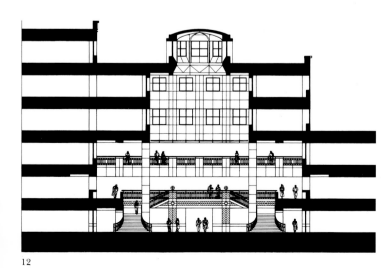

12

14

15

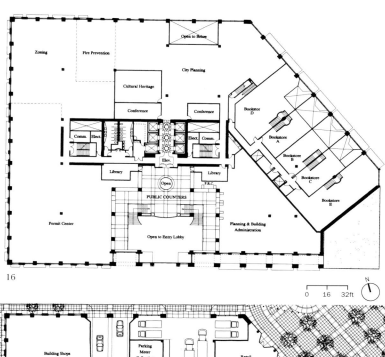

16

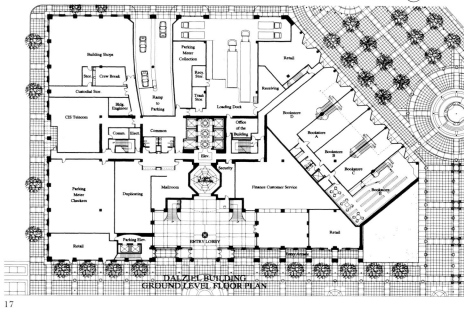

17

15 Model view through plaza
16 Second floor plan
17 First floor plan
18 Model view of plaza from above
19 Model view through plaza

0   16   32ft

N

18

19

DIA Westin Hotel

Design 1996
Denver, Colorado
DIA Development Corporation
325,000 square feet
Steel frame, precast concrete
Architectural precast concrete, glass, granite,
stainless steel, gypsum, carpet

Fentress Bradburn adds to its landmark design for the Denver International Airport with this significant concept hotel. The DIA Westin Hotel's semicircular glazed facade encompasses the north end of the passenger terminal and spans the elevated walkway that carries passengers to Concourse A. Its intriguing views include arriving and departing aircraft and the vast expanse of the Colorado prairie and mountain landscapes beyond. The hotel's glazed exterior belies its mass as it dissolves into the undulating shapes of the passenger terminal roof.

The hotel's location is carefully selected for maximum convenience to the terminal. Situated on axis to the terminal and airfield, it provides maximum ease and comfort for travelers delayed by layovers or inclement weather.

The completed design contains 544 rooms and is planned as a full-service hotel with restaurants, shops, convention and banqueting facilities, entertainment and an executive business center.

1

2

3

4

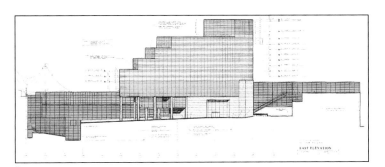

5

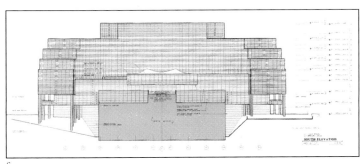

6

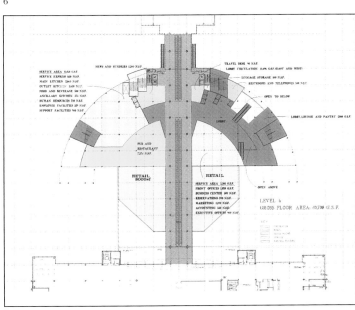

7

8

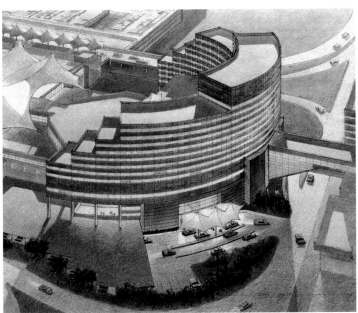

9

10

ICG Communications Corporate Headquarters

Design/Completion 1996/1997
Englewood, Colorado
ICG Communications Inc.
250,000 square feet
Composite steel frame, concrete core
Granite, glass, ceramic tiles, marble, metal, wood, carpet

Fentress Bradburn's new ICG Communications Corporate Headquarters building, in association with design architect Steven Wood, is located on a prime 16-acre site in the Inverness Business Park. Overlooking the Rocky Mountains' Front Range, the building's curved and canted facade is clad in glass and flame-cut polished granite. From the adjacent interstate highway, it provides an eye-catching drama, appearing to spill over the highway. From inside, it provides sweeping, panoramic vistas.

The eight-story building features a state-of-the-art communications command center with fiber-optic cabling and a two-story video screen viewable from the first floor lobby. The 280,000-square-foot plan is designed for 90 percent flexible open office space with 35,000 square feet of executive office space located on the top floor.

Landscaping has been carefully designed to fit within the Inverness master plan. A formal entry drive through landscaped terraces of trees provides a dramatic approach to the main entry. Although parking is provided on site, service and delivery have been placed at the lower level, completely hidden from view.

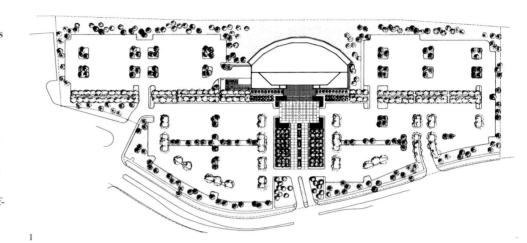

1

2

3

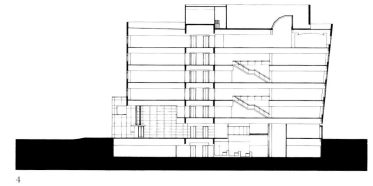

4

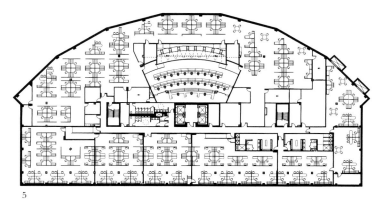

5

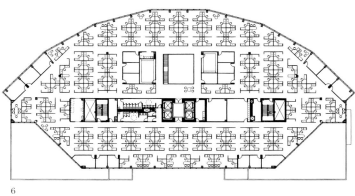

6

0   30   60ft

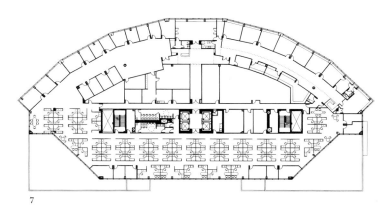

7

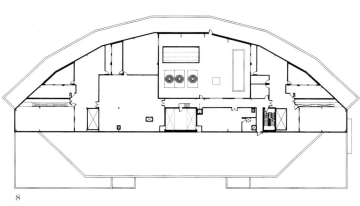

8

9

10

ICG Communications Corporate Headquarters   197

J.D. Edwards & Co. Corporate Headquarters

Design/Completion 1996/1997
Denver, Colorado
J.D. Edwards & Co.
216,000 square feet
Composite steel frame, concrete core
Architectural precast concrete, aluminum, mahogany,
granite, marble, glass

The new six-story J.D. Edwards & Co. Corporate Headquarters needed to accommodate the rapid growth of this global leader in developing enterprise-wide business applications for clients in a variety of industries, including construction, finance, government, mining and chemistry. The new facility, located in the Denver Technological Center, needed to be flexible while projecting an image of a confident corporate leader in multiple international fields.

The structure incorporates the latest developments in office building design, such as an open floor plan to accommodate systems furniture. One of the many client-related factors to be considered was the installation of a fiber-optic cabling system to allow for future expansion in the use of computers.

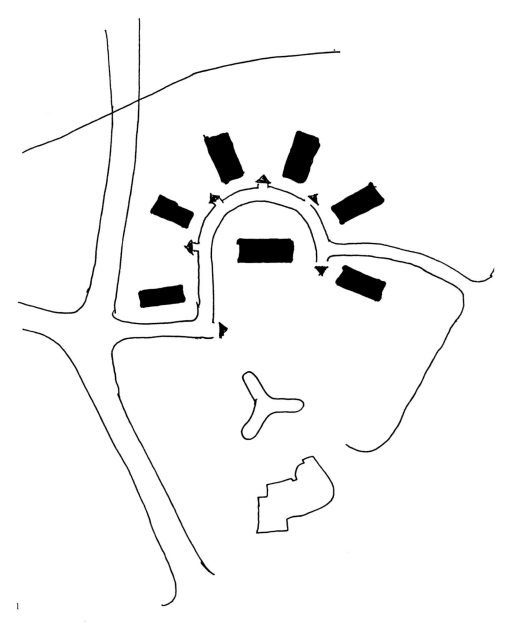

1

2

3

1 Concept sketch
2 Model: front elevation
3 Model: car park
4 First floor plan
5 Sixth floor plan

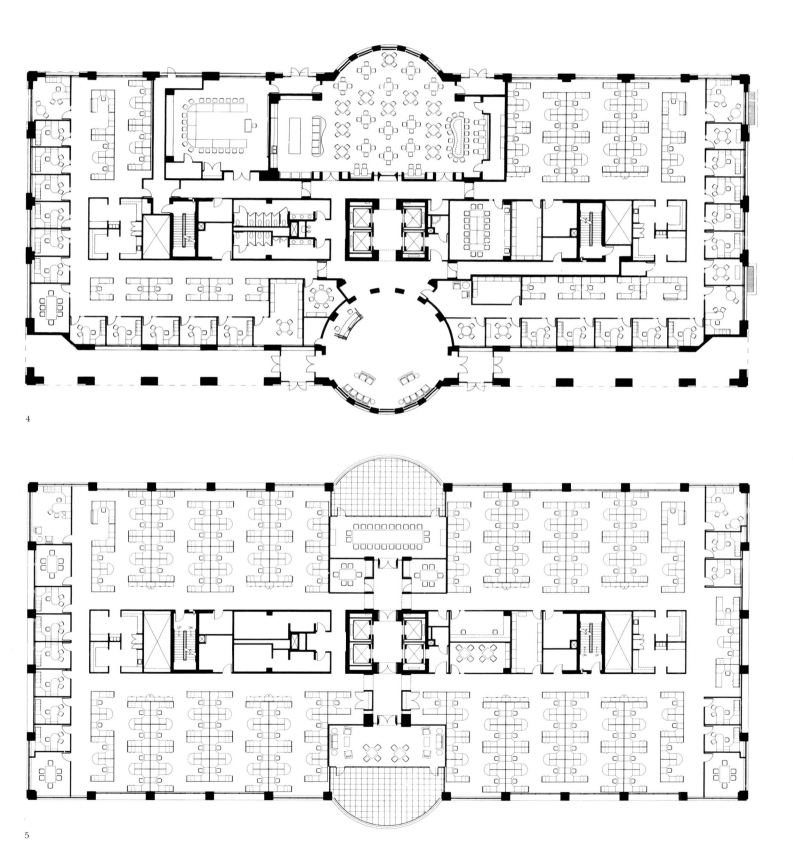

4

5

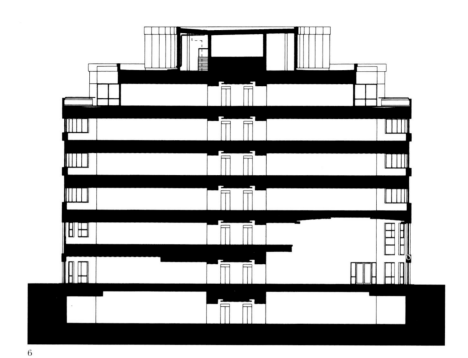

6

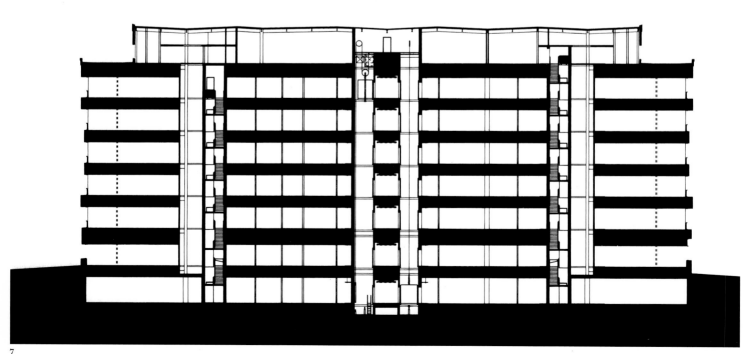

7

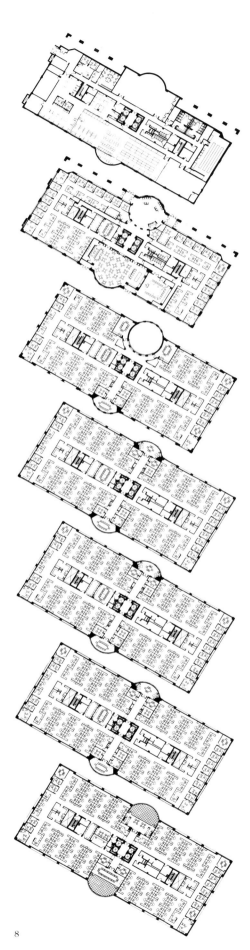

8

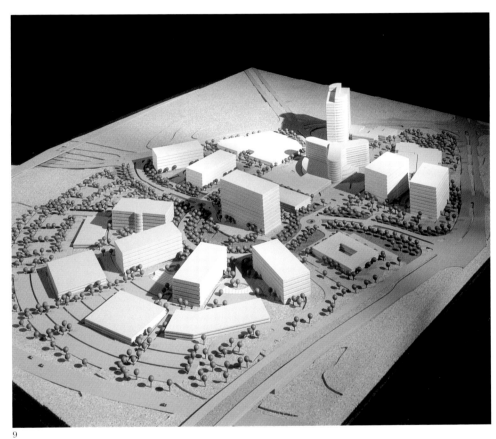

9

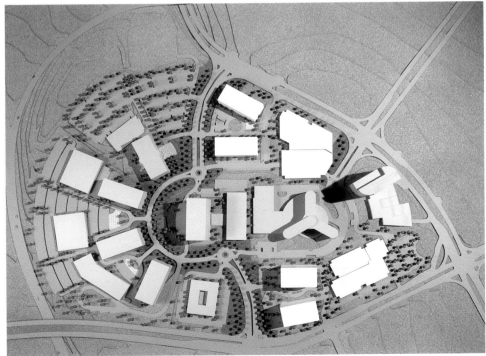

10

Gulf Canada Resources Limited

Design/Completion 1996/1997
Denver, Colorado
Gulf Canada Resources Limited
50,000 square feet
Wood, metal, custom furnishings, glass

The international operations headquarters of Gulf Canada Resources Limited is located on the top two floors of Philip Johnson's Norwest Bank Building in downtown Denver. This project was designed to accommodate Gulf's executive senior staff and support personnel, as well as their museum-quality Western art collection, *Spirit of the West*.

Gulf Canada commissioned Fentress Bradburn to create a space that provided a unique office environment, as well as an innovative space to display the art collection. The *Spirit of the West* collection was acquired by Gulf Canada to reflect the company's creativity, entrepreneurship and vision, and consists of Native American and cowboy artifacts. In response, Fentress Bradburn created a warm, comfortable, home-like atmosphere, which incorporates colors, materials and furnishings found within the western region of North America.

The design introduces textures and patterns that complement the collection. Walls are painted the color of wheat grass, recalling the Great Plains and providing a warm neutral background. Most of the flooring is five-inch-wide wood planks, which creates the perfect surface for displaying textiles. Wood doors, casings, crown moldings and base are unique details within the space. Hand-rubbed bronze hardware, column covers, stair railings, sinks, faucets, cabinet pulls and signage were created to look like hand-forged metal. Each finish material was selected for its handcrafted quality and simplicity.

Continued

1

2

1   Interior: window office
2   Interior: furnished wall

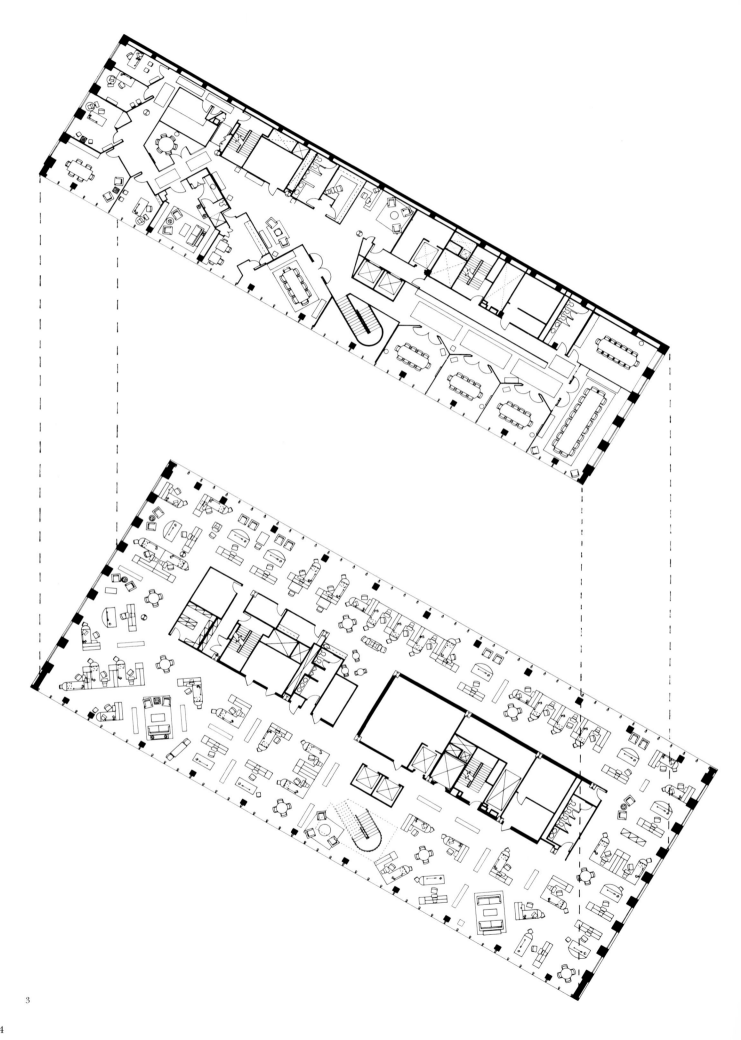

4

The 50th floor is designed as conference
space, while the floor below houses the
offices. The furnishings are predominantly
western or southwestern
in style, fabricated of leather, wood, or
bronze. Soft seating areas are located
throughout the space on both floors
to create a residential feeling and serve
as informal conference areas. Table lamps
and floor lamps provide a more intimate
lighting level. Custom office furniture is
fabricated out of wood with glass fronts.
In addition, custom bronze cabinet
pulls were designed with the Gulf logo.
The workstations are designed to meet
the specific needs of each work group:
executives, professionals and support staff.

Fentress Bradburn's unique experience
in creating comfortable and versatile
office environments as well as purposeful
museum spaces made this truly elegant
design possible.

3   Axonometric floor plans
4   Dining area

5

6

7

8

5   Waiting area
6   Corridor
7   Boardroom
8   General office
9   Inter-office stair

Clark County Master Plan

Design 1992
Las Vegas, Nevada
Clark County General Services Department
1,655,000 square feet

Fentress Bradburn won the national design competition to design and construct a government center for Clark County, Nevada. The competition also called for a master plan to include space for government administration, a law enforcement complex, a performing arts complex, a child-care facility and structured parking.

The government center, discussed earlier *(see page 134)*, draws upon Clark County's desert environment and regional history for inspiration.

The master plan centers on a 350,000-square-foot government administration complex that contains a single-story auditorium, a pyramid-shaped cafeteria and a cylindrical, six-story reception hall, as well as office buildings. The design physically embodies Clark County's philosophy of providing open, accessible government in a new civic cultural center. The bisected circular plan, detailed with a colonnade enclosing an amphitheater and a spine of evergreens, provides a centering device for the government building and subsequent additions.

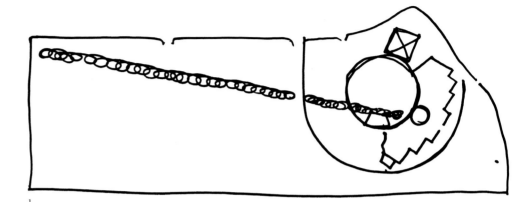

1

2

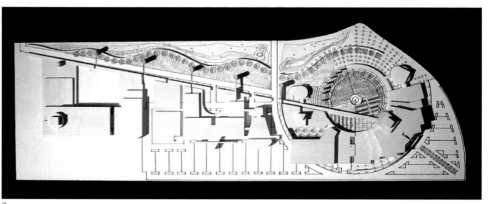

3

1   Concept sketch
2   Site plan model: aerial view
3   Model, Phase 1
4   Master site plan presentation board

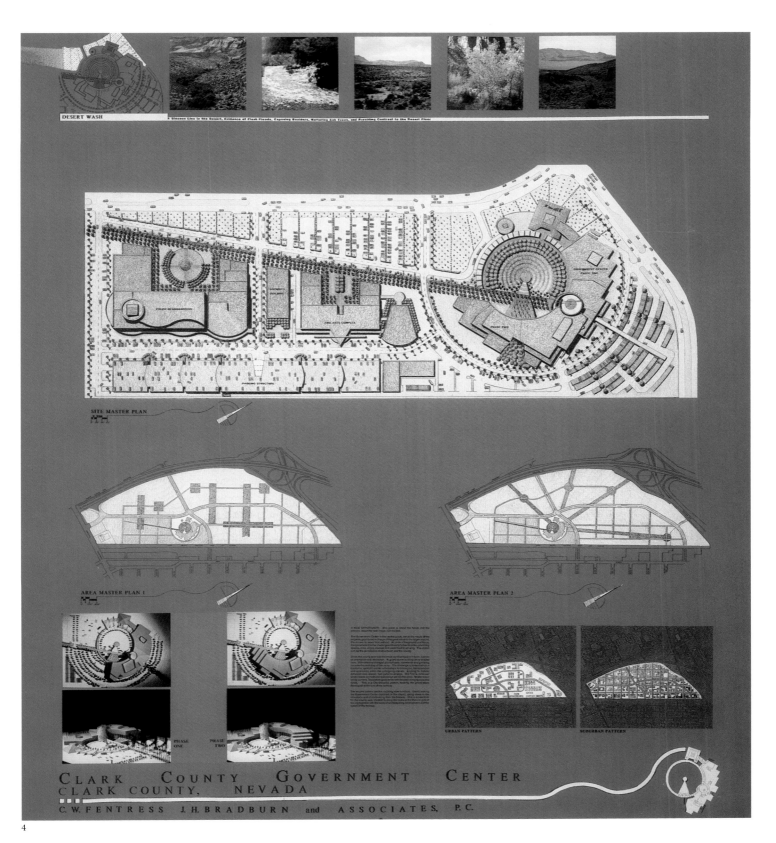

4

New Doha International Airport

Design/Completion 1996/2000
Doha, Qatar
Ministry of Municipal Affairs and Agriculture
900,000 square feet, 22 attached gates
Cast-in-place concrete, steel frame, sandstone,
architectural precast concrete
Sandstone, gypsum, carpet

Fentress Bradburn was the winner of an international design competition for the New Doha International Airport. The passenger terminal complex has two components: the land-side terminal, which contains all passenger processing facilities and land-side access points; and the air-side concourse, which contains all passenger waiting rooms and air-side access points for 22 attached aircraft gates and 8 hardstand positions.

The passenger terminal complex is made up of three levels. The first level (arrivals processing) of the land-side terminal contains all facilities for international passenger arrivals, including immigration, security checkpoints, baggage claim, customs facilities, a meeters and greeters hall and various support facilities.
The first level of the air-side concourse contains the baggage handling equipment, mechanical and electrical rooms, service areas and airline ground operations.

The second level of the air-side concourse contains the arrivals concourse leading to the arrivals processing area, a transfer passenger processing checkpoint, and an airport hotel for use by extended-stay transfer passengers. The remaining interstitial space is utilized for baggage distribution from the ticket counters and to the baggage claim devices, as well as mechanical, electrical and communications systems.

Continued

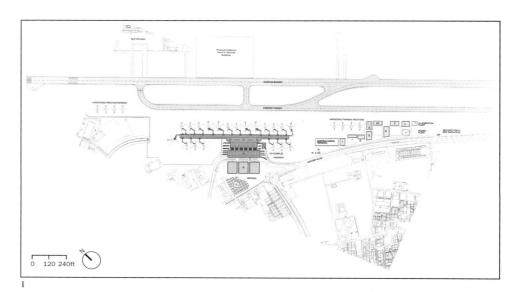

1

2

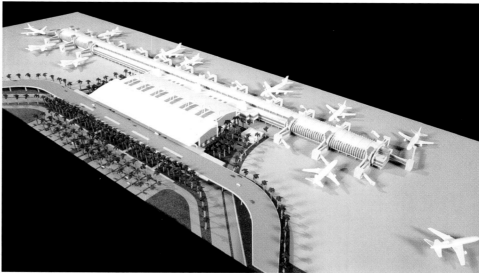

3

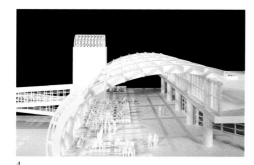

4

5

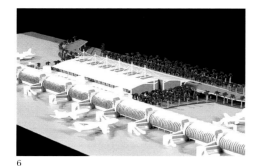

6

7

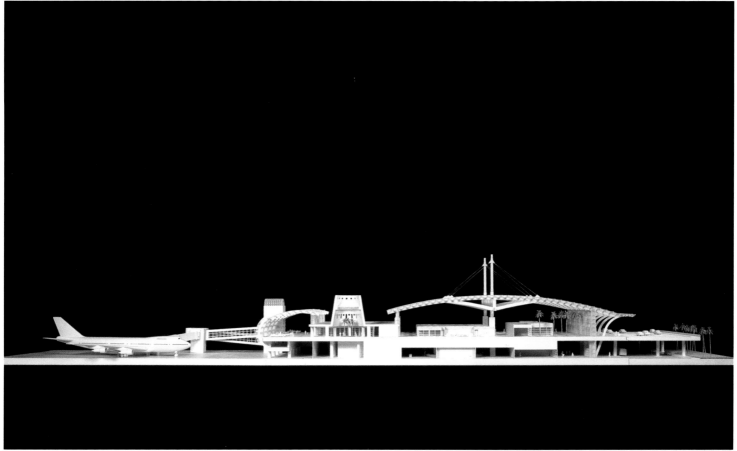

8

The third level (departures) of the land-side terminal contains all facilities for departing passenger processing functions, including the departures hall, security checkpoints, passenger check-in, outbound customs and immigration, retail and concessions. The third level of the air-side concourse contains all passenger waiting rooms, as well as enhanced duty-free concessions, giving the New Doha International Airport the premier duty-free facilities in the Middle East.

The design addresses both context and region, utilizing cultural and religious symbols drawn from Islam and from the local Qatari sailing vessels, *dhows*, to create an image that is at once recognizable and new.

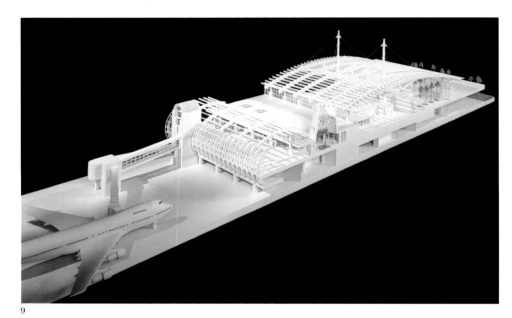

9

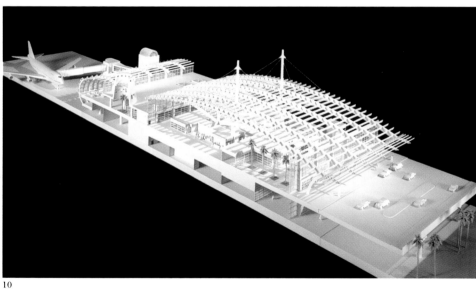

9   Model view from airside
10   Section model view from curbside
11&12   Day elevations
13   Axonometric view of levels one, two, and three

10

11

12

212

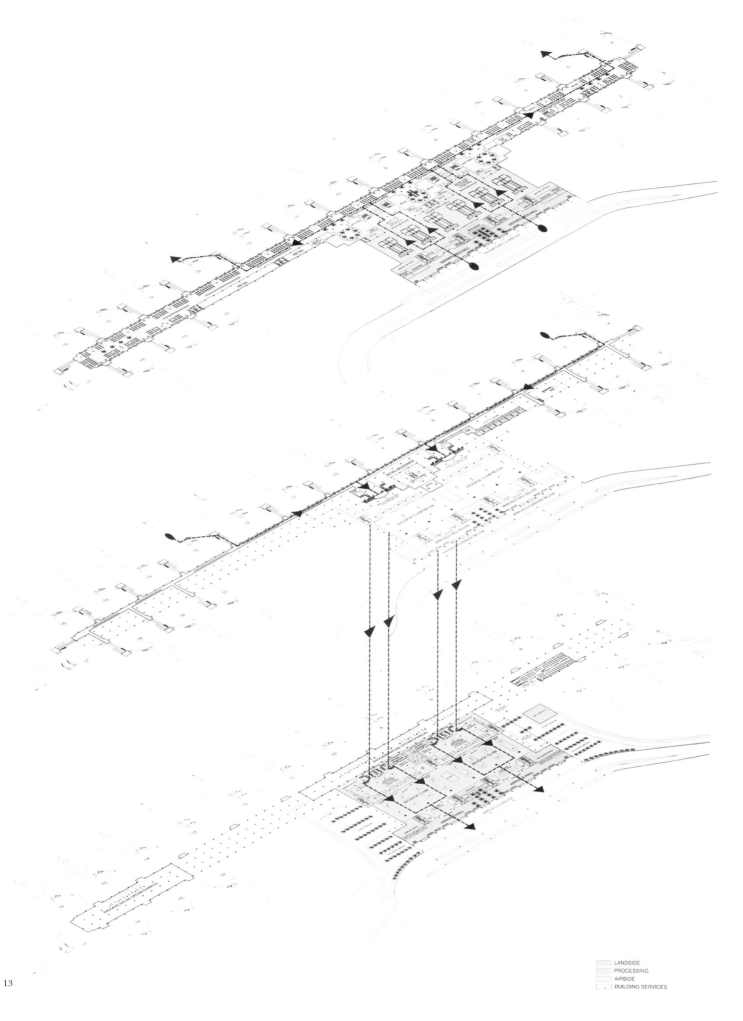

LANDSIDE
PROCESSING
AIRSIDE
BUILDING SERVICES

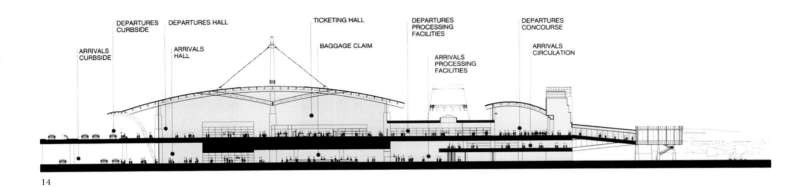

ARRIVALS
CURBSIDE

DEPARTURES
CURBSIDE

DEPARTURES HALL

ARRIVALS
HALL

TICKETING HALL

BAGGAGE CLAIM

DEPARTURES
PROCESSING
FACILITIES

ARRIVALS
PROCESSING
FACILITIES

DEPARTURES
CONCOURSE

ARRIVALS
CIRCULATION

14

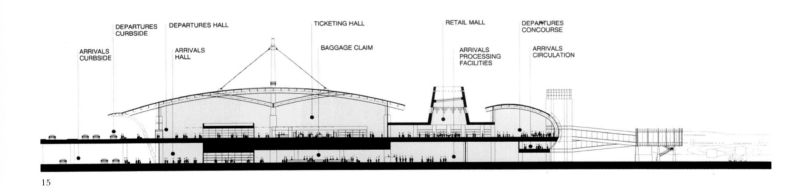

ARRIVALS
CURBSIDE

DEPARTURES
CURBSIDE

DEPARTURES HALL

ARRIVALS
HALL

TICKETING HALL

BAGGAGE CLAIM

RETAIL MALL

ARRIVALS
PROCESSING
FACILITIES

DEPARTURES
CONCOURSE

ARRIVALS
CIRCULATION

15

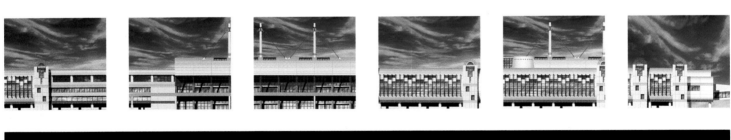

16

17

18

19

21

22

20 Departures concourse
21 Curbside
22 Departure hall

Larimer County Justice Center

Design/Completion 1997/2000
Fort Collins, Colorado
Larimer County, Colorado
79,150 square feet
Steel, concrete
Steel, brick, stone, architectural precast concrete,
glass, painted metal, gypsum, carpet

The architectural vernacular of Fort Collins and Larimer County is characterized by brick and stone masonry, horizontal string courses, deep, recessed openings, strong cornice lines and vertical forms marking important architectural elements. Repetitious fenestration patterns of vertically proportioned windows add additional strong horizontals. Urban buildings frequently have entrances at their corners, creating a strong diagonal emphasis in plan. The principal context for this project is made up of buildings with the characteristics mentioned above.

Fentress Bradburn's design for the courthouse, office and parking buildings contains vertically proportioned windows that create strong horizontal rhythms along the facade. These buildings are clad predominantly in brick with accents in stone and architectural precast concrete. The parking structure has been designed to mimic local retail and commercial office building proportions and fenestration patterns and has a high degree of finish detail in masonry, ornamental metals and glass at street level.

The courthouse is patterned in brick and stone on a stone base. Colored ornamental metal work, especially at the street and plaza level, and vaulted roofs express the functional relationships of the spaces within. The building steps back at the upper levels to maintain continuity of the street edge without overwhelming at the cornice line. Additionally, the vaulted roofs which cover the new courtrooms and jury deliberation suites evoke spatial proportions reminiscent of the Classical period. On the exterior, these forms recall the sweeping curves of the adjacent Saint Joseph School and the natural shape of Horsetooth Mountain.

1

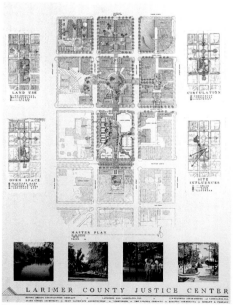

2

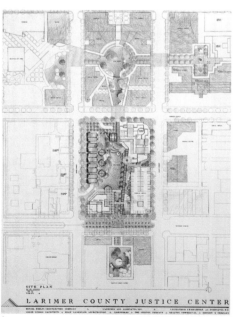

3

4

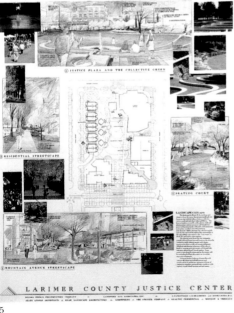

5

6

1 Model view
2 Master plan
3 Site plan
4 View of Justice Center from Civic Room
5&6 Landscape concept

COURTROOM ELEVATION

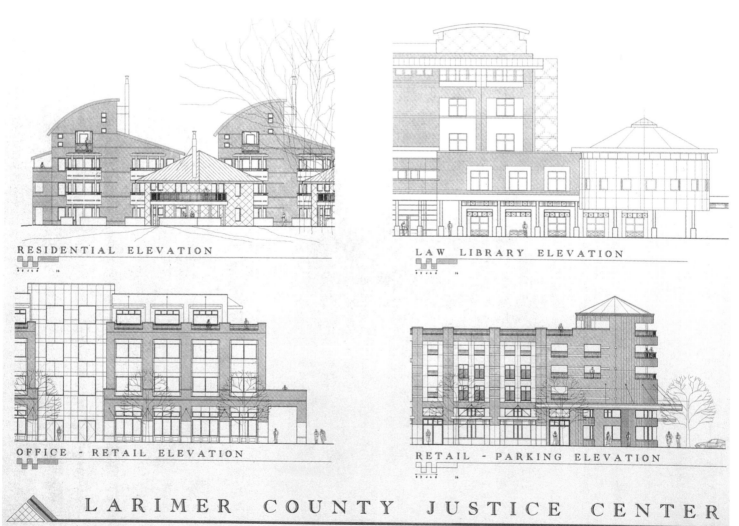

RESIDENTIAL ELEVATION

LAW LIBRARY ELEVATION

OFFICE - RETAIL ELEVATION

RETAIL - PARKING ELEVATION

LARIMER COUNTY JUSTICE CENTER

HENSEL PHELPS CONSTRUCTION COMPANY ▲ LANKFORD AND ASSOCIATES, INC. ▲ C.W.FENTRESS J.H.BRADBURN and ASSOCIATES, P.C.

ALLER LINGLE ARCHITECTS ▲ EDAW LANDSCAPE ARCHITECTURE ▲ LIGHTFORMS ▲ THE STEINER COMPANY ▲ REALTEC COMMERCIAL ▲ BIGELOW & COMPANY

7

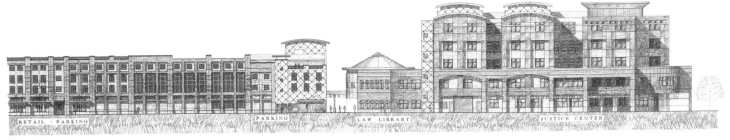

MASON STREET ELEVATION

RETAIL - PARKING · PARKING · LAW LIBRARY · JUSTICE CENTER

LAPORTE AVENUE ELEVATION

JUSTICE CENTER · CAFE · RESIDENTIAL

HOWES STREET ELEVATION

RESIDENTIAL · OFFICE - RETAIL

VIEW INSIDE CIVIC ROOM LOOKING SOUTH

PARKING · ARCADE · OFFICE - RETAIL

LARIMER COUNTY JUSTICE CENTER

HENSEL PHELPS CONSTRUCTION COMPANY △ LANKFORD AND ASSOCIATES, INC. △ C.W. FENTRESS J.H. BRADBURN and ASSOCIATES, P.C.
ALLER LINGLE ARCHITECTS △ EDAW LANDSCAPE ARCHITECTURE △ LIGHTFORMS △ THE STEINER COMPANY △ REALTEC COMMERCIAL △ BIGELOW & COMPANY

8

7 Detail elevations
8 Elevations

Goldrush Casino

Design/Completion 1997/2000
Central City, Colorado
Dynasty Corporation Hotel and Casino
60,000 square feet
Steel, concrete
Wood, metal roofing, metal siding, plaster,
carpet, tiles

Fentress Bradburn's design for the
Goldrush Casino captures the essence
of Central City's heyday as a 19th-century
gold-mining town. Since then it had
become almost a ghost town, until recently
revitalized by the Colorado gaming
industry. In the wake of tremendous
growth have come such urban problems as
congestion, inadequate parking and lack
of architectural focus. This purely regional
design addresses many of these issues.

Proper siting reduces congestion, and
adjacent parking will alleviate some of the
town's traffic problems. Additional
architectural focus is given to the town
through the casino's elevation, which
mimics the area's historic mining
buildings. This concept ties the building
more closely to its regional neighbors than
to the new entertainment industry
construction in the town. Several historic
buildings on the site are also preserved
and restored.

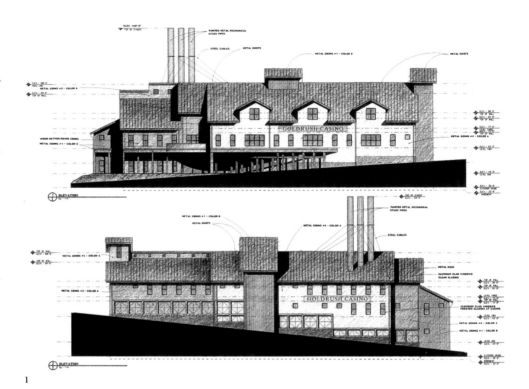

1

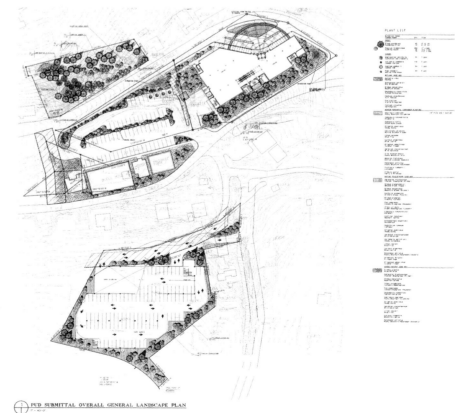

PUD SUBMITTAL OVERALL GENERAL LANDSCAPE PLAN

2

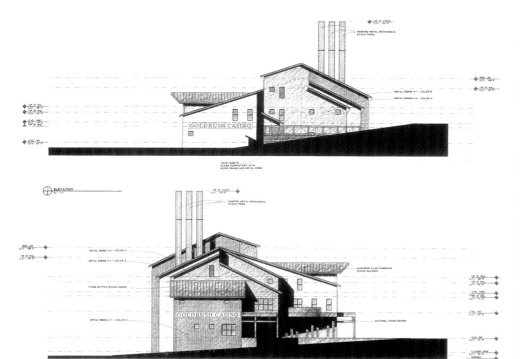

1   Elevations
2   General site plan
3   Elevations
4&5   Casino model views
6   Site plan
7   Frontier Town elevation

Deira Bus Station and Car Park

Design/Completion 1997/2000
Dubai, United Arab Emirates
Dubai Municipality
944,881 square feet
Steel, concrete
Steel, architectural precast concrete, stone, ceramic tiles,
plaster, wood, carpet, glass

The architectural language established for the New Deira Bus Station and multi-story car park is derived from the rich cultural and architectural heritage of Dubai. This language is not mimetic, but is consciously influenced by local context. In addition to innovative technical elements, such as the structural truss system over the bus plaza, the spaces are defined by a new expression of architecture that combines dramatic spaces with functionality. The roof trusses define the bus plaza as a unique environment, while the roof itself offers shaded space with diffuse lighting, similar to the shaded courtyards of Dubai.

Details are functional and not merely ornamental. This approach permits cultural ornament to be expressed in the design solutions to minor problems such as creating window grills that serve as shade screens. Vertical elements of wind towers, watchtowers and minarets are used as the structural buttresses which support the roof trusses over the bus plaza. These elements house the exit stairs and elevators of the car park as well as providing cooling.

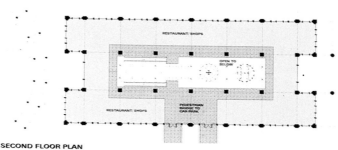

SECOND FLOOR PLAN
SCALE 1:200

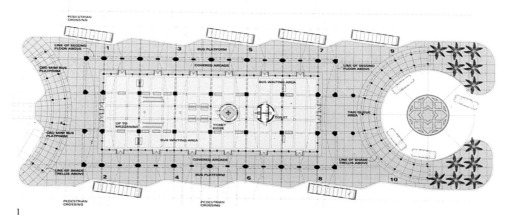

1

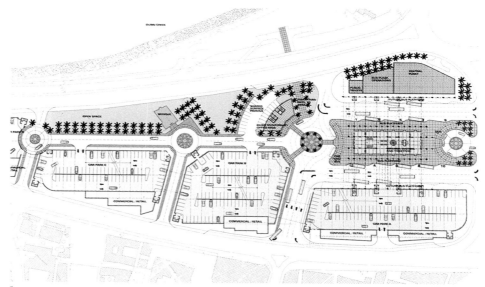

2

1   Typical first floor and second floor plans
2   Site plan
3   Typical upper level plan
4&5 Site analysis
6   Typical concept studies
7   Section and elevation
8   Elevations

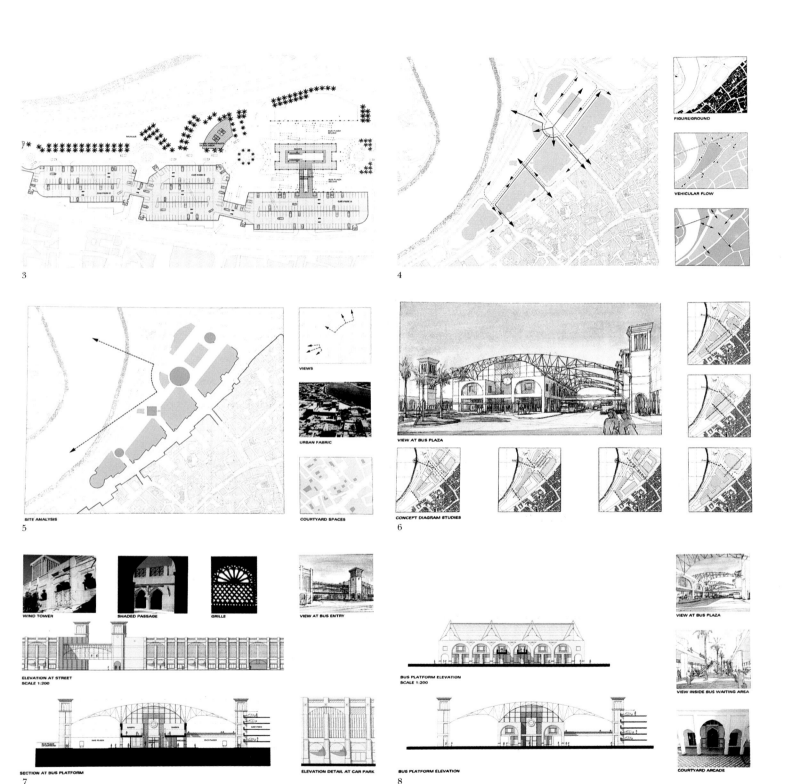

3

4

FIGURE/GROUND

VEHICULAR FLOW

5

VIEWS

URBAN FABRIC

COURTYARD SPACES

SITE ANALYSIS

6

VIEW AT BUS PLAZA

CONCEPT DIAGRAM STUDIES

7

WIND TOWER

SHADED PASSAGE

GRILLE

VIEW AT BUS ENTRY

VIEW AT BUS PLAZA

ELEVATION AT STREET
SCALE 1:200

BUS PLATFORM ELEVATION
SCALE 1:200

VIEW INSIDE BUS WAITING AREA

SECTION AT BUS PLATFORM

ELEVATION DETAIL AT CAR PARK

8

BUS PLATFORM ELEVATION

COURTYARD ARCADE

Palmetto Bay Plantation Villas

Design/Completion 1996/1999
Camp Bay–Port Royal, Roatan, Honduras
Roatan Development Group
4,792,000 square feet (site area); 45 residential units
Concrete, wood
Concrete, wood, tropical hardwood, gypsum, stone tiles

Palmetto Bay Plantation is a mixed-use resort development on Roatan Island, located in the western Caribbean off the coast of Honduras. The site has a beautiful white sand beach with a backdrop of steep hillsides covered with tropical vegetation. Several varieties of tropical trees, such as banana, coconut, mango and cashew cover the site. The water is clear and warm with a large coral barrier reef about 600 feet offshore.

The architecture was designed to reflect aspects of local traditional building, to respond to the tropical environment and to enhance the visitor's island experience. Raised structures with deep overhangs and louvered walls allow for maximum natural ventilation and optimize views. Features such as louvered doors, lattice work, transoms and high ceilings capitalize on natural breezes while providing daylight and ventilation for every room. Smaller areas such as closets, bathrooms and pantries, are also well-ventilated to minimize moisture and prevent mildew. Each hotel room has its own observation deck that provides guests with dramatic views of the natural landscape, gardens and sea.

Recognizing that Palmetto Bay is located in one of the world's greatest natural environments, Fentress Bradburn aimed to preserve and enhance existing natural features. Their primary commitment was to provide a model of environmentally sustainable architectural development for the island of Roatan. The result enhances natural features by preserving steep hills, wetlands, and drainage basins and returning vegetation to its natural tropical forest condition. Tropical hardwoods certified by the Rain Forest Alliance were used and detailed in ways reflecting the tropical setting.

Continued

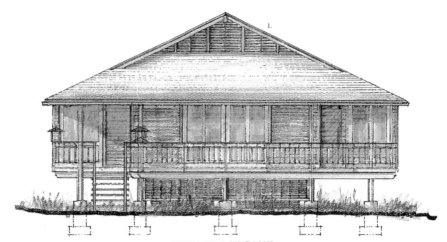

ELEVATION OF CASTIA

PALMETTO BAY PLANTATION
C.W. Fentress J.H. Bradburn and Associates, P.C.
PLANS ARE SUBJECT TO FUTURE DEVELOPMENT

LEGEND
1. Louvered Ventilation Area
2. Deck Area
3. Concrete Foundation

1

2

1 Elevation of Castia
2 Beach rendering
3 Rendered site plan

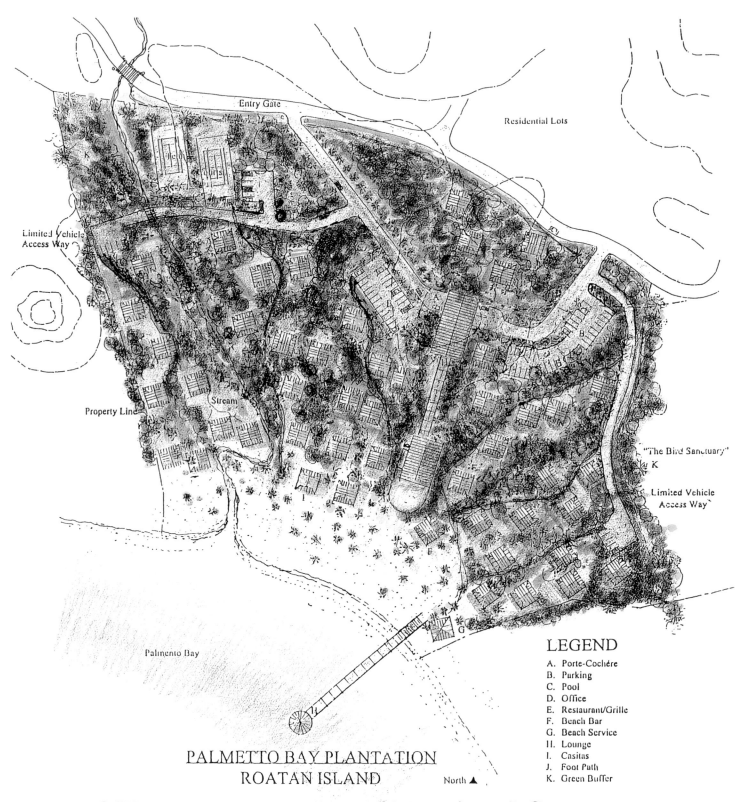

LEGEND

A. Porte-Cochére
B. Parking
C. Pool
D. Office
E. Restaurant/Grille
F. Beach Bar
G. Beach Service
H. Lounge
I. Casitas
J. Foot Path
K. Green Buffer

Entry Gate

Residential Lots

Limited Vehicle Access Way

Property Line

Stream

"The Bird Sanctuary" K

Limited Vehicle Access Way

Palmetto Bay

North ▲

PALMETTO BAY PLANTATION
ROATAN ISLAND

C.W. Fentress J.H. Bradburn and Associates, P.C.

3

4

5

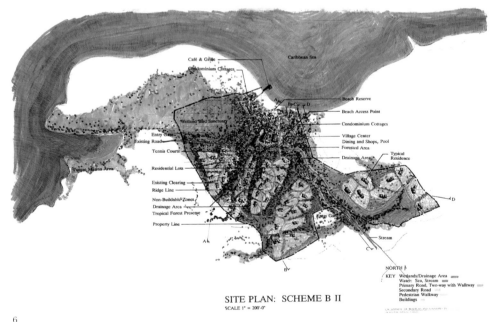

Café & Grille
Condominium Cottages
Caribbean Sea
Beach Reserve
Beach Access Point
Wetland Bird Sanctuary
Condominium Cottages
Entry Gate
Existing Road
Village Center
Dining and Shops, Pool
Forested Area
Tennis Courts
Drainage Area
Typical Residence
Residential Lots
Future Marina Area
Existing Clearing
Ridge Line
Non-Buildable Zones
Drainage Area
Tropical Forest Preserve
Property Line
Entry Gate
Stream

NORTH
KEY Wetlands/Drainage Area
Water: Sea, Stream
Primary Road, Two-way with Walkway
Secondary Road
Pedestrian Walkway
Buildings

SITE PLAN: SCHEME B II
SCALE 1" = 200'-0"

6

Palmetto Bay Villa's architecture consists
of contextual and regional expressions
drawn from the best elements of the Bay
Island's vernacular architecture. The
present-day homes on the island are a
synthesis of indigenous influences and the
architectural heritages of the peoples who
have historically settled the islands. These
vary from English colonial and American
Victorian to the handcrafted houses of
barbecue (braided twigs) built by the early
Paya Indians and Africans.

4   View of beach model
5   View of beach model plan
6   Master plan of entire resort

7

7   Restaurant model
Opposite:
    View of restaurant model from ocean

FIRM PROFILE

Biographies

Curtis Worth Fentress FAIA, RIBA
Principal in Charge of Design

Curtis W. Fentress received a Bachelor of Architecture degree in 1972 from North Carolina State University's School of Design, where he graduated at the top of his class. While in residence, he was awarded an AIA–AIAF Fellowship (1970), a Graham Foundation Fellowship (1971), and the Alpha Rho Chi Medal, the highest honor bestowed on a designer by an architectural school (1972).

After graduation, Mr. Fentress joined the New York firm of I.M. Pei and Partners (1972–1977) where he worked on several international projects, including the Raffles Place Center in Singapore. As a project designer for Kohn Pedersen Fox of New York (1977–1980), he was responsible for designing the Amoco Building in Denver, Colorado, a composition for which he was awarded *Building Design and Construction* magazine's Young Professional of the Year award in 1980. In January of 1980, Mr. Fentress formed C.W. Fentress and Associates.

Renamed in 1989, C.W. Fentress J.H. Bradburn and Associates P.C., is now the largest architectural firm in Colorado and employs approximately 100 people. The practice is both national and international, with projects in more than a dozen states of the U.S.A., as well as the Middle East, the Commonwealth of Independent States (the former Soviet Union), Central America and Korea. The firm has won more than 122 awards, including 45 from the American Institute of Architects since 1980.

As principal in charge of design, Mr. Fentress has directed the design of a variety of large-scale public sector projects within Colorado, including the passenger terminal complex of the new Denver International Airport, the Colorado Convention Center, 1999 Broadway, and the Jefferson County Government Center.

Outside of Colorado, his project list includes several national and international competition-winning designs: the National Museum of Wildlife Art in Jackson, Wyoming; the Clark County Government Center in Las Vegas, Nevada; the Natural Resources Laboratory and Administration Building in Olympia, Washington; the National Cowboy Hall of Fame in Oklahoma City, Oklahoma; the New Inchon International Airport in Seoul, Republic of South Korea and the Howard Hughes Development Corporate Office Building in Las Vegas, Nevada. Most recently, the firm was selected as the winner of international design competitions for the City of Oakland Administration Buildings in California and the Doha International Airport in Qatar.

Mr. Fentress's work has been cited in *Curtis Worth Fentress* (Milan, Italy: L'Arca Edizioni spa, 1995), *Fentress Bradburn Architects* (Washington, DC: Studio Press, 1995), *Retrospective of Courthouse Design: 1980–1991* (Williamsburg, Virginia: National Center for State Courts, 1992), and *American Architecture: The State of the Art in the 80s* (Ashland, Kentucky: Hanover Publishing Co., 1985).

At present, Mr. Fentress is licensed in 19 States and the District of Columbia, and he was the 1993 President of the Colorado Chapter of the AIA. As a member of the Royal Institute of British Architects, the American Institute of Architects, the Ontario Association of Architects, the Urban Land Institute, Urban Design Forum and as a mentor of the keen young architectural mind, Mr. Fentress continues to lecture widely and serve as a visiting critic at colleges and universities across the United States.

James Henry Bradburn AIA
Principal in Charge of Production

James H. Bradburn was born in Rochester, New York. He received a Bachelor of Building Science degree in 1966 and a Bachelor of Architecture degree in 1967 from Rensselaer Polytechnic Institute, where he earned distinction as both an athlete and a scholar. Described as "an architect with the heart of an engineer," Mr. Bradburn has consistently sought to improve production performance and architectural technology by rigorously applying the precepts of science to innovative technical solutions and materials application.

Mr. Bradburn has been a practicing architect since 1967, is licensed in several States, and is a member of the American Institute of Architects and the National Council of Architectural Registration Boards. He also maintains a membership in the American Arbitration Association, the Construction Specifications Institute, the American Concrete Institute, and the American Society for Testing and Materials. Mr. Bradburn is an early member of the Design-Build Institute of America, a member of its policy and process committee and of the manual of practice task force, and a frequent lecturer on the topic of design-build at professional seminars.

In 1981, Mr. Bradburn pioneered the West's first design incorporating four-sided silicone adhesive glazing using insulating glass. In the same year, he developed a 30-foot-long prestressed limestone spandrel system, allowing natural stone to be used economically for a 43-story high-rise exterior. The following year Mr. Bradburn devised a system for a "building within a building," enabling a historic building (circa 1886) to provide the constantly maintained levels of temperature, humidity and cleanliness necessary to house a $40 million Western art collection. Between 1989 and 1990, Mr. Bradburn proposed the use of fabric and directed the production for the largest fully enclosed tensile membrane structure in the world,

at Denver International Airport. This project also utilized Mr. Bradburn's innovative epoxy-impregnated fiber-reinforced natural granite flooring solution in the world's largest installation of this material. Mr. Bradburn also explored innovative bidding procedures for large applications of natural stone masonry in Las Vegas's $48 million County Government Center. The 1990s saw Fentress Bradburn setting the benchmark for indoor environmental standards in Washington State's Natural Resources Building, commissioned through a national competition.

In addition to his technically driven solutions, he strives to create a balance of ego and expertise with effective mentoring aimed at "hearing all voices" and instilling individual self-esteem thus "allowing good things to come forth." Mr. Bradburn's advocacy of streamlined project management led the firm to install the region's most sophisticated CADD system in 1981. He optimized its use with an internal LAN and external WAN for all employees that today offers a comprehensive catalogue of resources, project details, technical solutions and office and world-wide communications.

Mr. Bradburn's sensitivity to the need for teamwork and constructive cooperation on multifaceted design projects has led him to become a strong advocate for partnership building. His series of regional lectures on project partnering and team building was published in *Partnering in Design and Construction* (McGraw-Hill, 1995). He has also had several significant technological articles published, including "New Attachment Technique: Alternative to Traditional Stone Cladding Systems," which appeared in *Modern Steel Construction* in 1981.

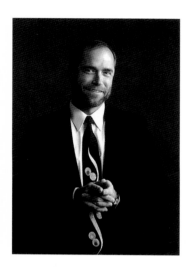

Michael O. Winters AIA
Principal

Michael Winters was born in Chicago, Illinois. He received a Bachelor of Science in Architecture degree with high honors from the University of Wisconsin at Milwaukee in 1977, and a Master of Architecture degree from the University of Colorado at Denver in 1980. While at the University of Wisconsin, Mr. Winters was awarded a scholarship to study architecture in London during the 1977 academic year.

During his graduate studies at the University of Colorado, he received a national design award from the Prestressed Concrete Institute, and was awarded the 1979–1980 Thesis Design Award, the 1980 AIA Certificate of Merit Scholarship Award and the 1980 AIA School Medal Award.

Mr. Winters has been a visiting critic and lecturer at the School of Architecture and Planning of the University of Colorado in Denver and Boulder. He is a member of the Denver Hispanic Chamber of Commerce and the Advisory Board in Denver. He served as awards chairman for the Colorado Chapter of the American Institute of Architects in 1989 and the Western Mountain Region of the AIA in 1990.

Mr. Winters worked with Skidmore, Owings and Merrill (1978–1981) prior to joining C.W. Fentress and Associates in 1981. He became the firm's first associate, the first senior associate, the first associate principal, and now serves as a principal. He has been the team leader for the firm's largest and most complex projects, including the Denver International Airport Passenger Terminal Complex, Clark County Government Center, Colorado Convention Center, Idaho Power Company Corporate Headquarters, Tucson City Center Master Plan and 1999 Broadway. His work has been featured in numerous publications and has received 20 design awards, including seven from the American Institute of Architects.

Ronald R. Booth AIA
Principal

Ronald Booth was born in Manhattan, Kansas, in 1946 and received a Bachelor of Architecture degree from the University of Kansas in 1973.

He has been a project architect with C.W. Fentress J.H. Bradburn and Associates P.C. since 1988. Prior to joining the firm, Mr. Booth was an associate principal with CCSB Architects in Denver, Colorado (1982–1988), and a vice president with RNL Inc., also in Denver (1973–1982).

As a project architect and design studio team leader for more than 25 years, Mr. Booth has acquired a broad range of experience with practically every building type. His national competition-winning designs include the Natural Resources Laboratory and Administration Building for the State of Washington at the Capitol in Olympia (Award of Merit, Architecture and Energy, Portland Chapter of the American Institute of Architects, 1993; Award of Merit, Gold Nugget Awards, Pacific Coast Builders' Conference and *Builder* magazine, 1993; and Grand Award, Gold Nugget Awards, Pacific Coast Builders' Conference and *Builder* magazine, 1993); the National Cowboy Hall of Fame and Western Heritage Museum in Oklahoma City, Oklahoma and a new administrative and government office complex for the City of Oakland, California.

Recently, Mr. Booth has lead design teams on an office and laboratory building for the General Services Administration to house the National Oceanic and Atmospheric Administration in Boulder, Colorado and for the J.D. Edwards & Co. Corporate Headquarters in Denver, as well as for international design competitions for airports in Madrid, Spain and Tenerife, Canary Islands.

Mr. Booth has been on the juries of numerous awards programs and design competitions and is a member of the American Institute of Architects.

Associates and Collaborators

Principals
Curtis Worth Fentress
James Henry Bradburn
Michael O. Winters
Ronald R. Booth

Associate Principals
John M. Kudrycki
Brian Chaffee
Jack M. Mousseau
Thomas J. Walsh

Senior Associates
Jeffrey W. Olson
Mark A. Wagner
Ned Kirschbaum

Associates
Todd R. Britton
Jayne Coburn
Gregory R. Gidez
Karen Gilbert
Robert Louden
John Wurzenberger, Jr.

Collaborators
Ana Acosta
Luis O. Acosta
Don Adams
Mary Adkins
Deborah R. Allen
Lyle R. Anderson
Jacqueline Y. April
Judy Arkulari
David Arnoth
Debbie Atencio
Robin Ault
LeAlta Ayers
Galen Bailey
Antoinette Colonel Baines
Mary Baird
B. Edward Balkin
Linda I. Barclay
Melissa Bare
Jennifer Barry
Margorie Bates
Karen Bauman
Nina Bazian
Nina Beardsley

Karen R. Beasley
Brian Beckler
Benjamin Berg
Jane Bertschinger
Gregory Biggs
Gregory D. Billingham
Susan Blosten
Amanda Bonsante
Blake Booth
James M. Boucher
Betty Lou Bowers
Barbara Bowman
Bill Bramblett
Sandy Brand
Daniel Braun
Charlotte C. Breed
Amy Brennan
Kerry Briggs
Mark Brinkman
Rosanne Brock
Robert T. Brodie
Andrew Bromberg
Russell Brown
Kristine Brundige
Carla Brunstead
Elizabeth Buckman
Nora Buriks
Richard Burkett
Robert Busch
William Buyers
David Caldwell
Katharine Capra
Peter D. Carlson
James Carney
James Carpenter
Carol A. Carr
Christopher A. Carvell
Gary Chamer
Roger A. Chandler
Marilynn Charles
Deborah Chelemes
Danielle Cheverez
Garrett M. Christnacht
Arpie Christianian Chucovich
Andrew Clements
Roslyn Clinton
Shannon Cody
Michelle A. C. Coffman
Melanie Colcord

Martin Cole
Jacqueline Collard
Melora Collette
Pamela Combs
John Conklin
Sonia Rocio Contreras
Jack Cook
Cheryl Cooper
Vicky Cooper
Ruth Cramer
Judi Cross
Delores Cuba
Jennifer Cuney
Ava Dahlstrom
Carl J. Dalio
Eric Dalio
Kristin Halstrum Danford
James Daniels
Robert G. Datson
Philip Davis
Donald W. DeCoster
Janet Delaney
Joanne Delude
Lawrence Depenbusch
Kimberly Devore
Douglas Dick
Marc Dietrick
Dalas Disney
MaryJane Donovan
Petr Dostal
Mary Claire Downing
Nicole Downing
Michael Driscoll
Catherine Dunn
Diane Duran
Douglas Eichelberger
Michael Eltrich
Annette English
Brian Erickson
Rafael Espinoza
Kristine K. Ewoldt
Catherine Faulkner
Carolyn S. Fedler
Ray Fedler
Coleen Fisher
Margaret Fisher
Robert Fitzgerald
Josephine Flanagan
Melinda Florian

Ellen Flynn-Heapes
Lewis Fowler
Frank Fritz
Steven Fritzky
Peter Frothingham
Lisa K. Fudge
Marie Fulop
J. Scott Gabel
John Gagnon
Marjorie A. Gallion
Kathleen Corner Galvin
Michael Gengler
Haia Ghalib
Linda Ghannam
Ali Gidfar
Mitchell Lee Gilbert
Deborah Gisburne
Dawn Givens
Edward Goewert
Ken Goff
Mitchell Gomez
David Gorman
Roxanne Gorrell
John Gossett
Stanley Gould
Andrea Grant
Jean L. Greaves
Randy Green
Stephen O. Gregory
Susan Griffith
Robert C. Grubbs
Gregory J. Guastella
D'Anne Gudeman
Jan Gustafson
Renata Hajek
Christie Halverson-Larson
Elizabeth Hamilton
Timothy Hanagan
David Hardee
David Harmon
Mark T. Harpe
Frederic M. Harrington
Geoffrey B. Harris
Milan Hart
James F. Hartman
William Haskey
Ala F. Hason
Frank G. Hege
JoAnne Hege

Michael Henry
Richard A. Herbert
Sheryl Highsmith
Erin Hillhouse
Bridget Hilton
Kimble Hobbs
Barbara K. Hochstetler
Warren Hogue III
Kevan Hoertdoerfer
Kimberly J. Holmes
Brian Homerding
Jon Hooley
Laurie Horn
Ernest W. Howard
Arthur A. Hoy III
June Huhn
Doris Hung
Kristen Hurty
Lisa Jelliffe
Charles Johns
Bret Johnson
James Johnson
Kelly J. Johnson
Lyn Wisecarver Johnson
Greg Jones
Glenda Jordan
Judith Jump
J. Mike Klebba
Anthia Kappos
Jeff M. Kaufman
Kathy Diane Kavan
Jeffrey Keast
Patrick Keefe
Andrew Kelmers
Nancy Kettner
Michael Kicklighter
Earl John Kincaid
Angeline C. Kinnaird
Mary Jane Koenig
Loretta Konrad
Kathleen Krenzer
Stan Kulesa
Barbara Kusske
Jamie LaCasse
Rene L. Lancaster
Bere Lane
Erin Lee
Lauren Lee
Linda Lee

Greg Lemon
Joan Lerch
Leslie Leydorf
Forrest A. Liles
Gregory Lockridge
Harold O. Love
Deborah Lucking
Christoph B. Lueder
Randy E. Macmillan
Robin Mahaffey
Renee Major
Sanjeev Malhotra
Colleen Marcus
J. Scott Martin
John L. Mason
Karin Mason
Sally Mason
Brent Mather
John K. McCauley
Carla L. McConnell
John M. McGahey
Loren McGlone
Cydney McGlothlin
Mark McGlothlin
Patrick M. McKelvey
Daniel F. McLaughlin
Geeta Mehta
Cynthia Melton
Julia Mendelson
David Miller
Michael Miller
Pam Mills
Francis Mishler
Doni Mitchell
Mona Mohney
Irina Mokrova
Sanjeev Molhatra
Daniel L. Monger
Wilbur Moore
Gary Morris
Ned Morris
Bruce R. Mosteller
Rodney Mowry
Jacqueline Murray
Richard D. Myers
Dan Naegele
Sonja Natter
James Niemi
Minh (Mark) Nguyen

Associates and Collaborators continued

Kathy Nightengale
Lyn K. Oda
Marnie Odegard
Clement Okoye
A. Chris Olson
Christian Olson
Brian Ostler
Kathy O'Donnell
Robert J. O'Donnell
James W. O'Neill
Mark Outman
Teri Paris
Michel Pariseau
Wee Park
Wendy Paulson
Beverly G. Pax
Frederick R. Pax
Maria Pelayo-Loza
John Petro
W. Harrison Phillips
Elisabeth Post
Dorothy Potter
Gary Prager
Susan Pratt
Brit Probst
Sandy Prouty
Gerard Prus
Clay Pryor
Michelle Ray
Robert Reedy
Renae Richards
Heather Richardson
Sherri Riepe
Robert Riffel
Shannon Riley
Penelope Roberts
Blaine Rodgers
David Robb
Kristen Rogers
John Rollo
Brigette Rothfuss-Moore
Mark Rothman
Robert Root
William Rosebrook
Lou Ann Roses
Tanya Roumph
Tim Roush
Raymond L. Rupert
Kelly Rutherford

Alexander S. Ryou
Janice M. Sadar
Robin Sakahara
John M. Salisbury
Kevin Sawchuck
Carol Scheibe
Ray Schelgunov
Laura M. Schumacher
Stuart A. Schunck
Tymmie Serr
Anthony F. Serratore
Lisa Shelton
Jyh-Lin Michael Shen
Aleksandr Sheykhet
Catherine Shields
Valerie Slack
Harold T. Small
Carol Ann Smith
Jill Smith
Stephanie Smith
Jim Snyder
James Sobey
Amy Solomon
Joseph Solomon
Jessica Sommers
Christy Sorrese
Joy Spatz
Eric A. Spielman
John J. Stein
Michael Stesney
Byron Stewart
Maggie Stienstra
Carolyn S. Stojeba
Kristoffer Strain
Donald Strum
Les Stuart
Leslie Sudders
Voraporn (Mai) Sundarupura
Randy Swanson
Nathaniel A. Taiwo
Alexa Taylor
John R. Taylor
Thomas P. Theobald
Alex Thomé
Debbie Thurgood
David Tompkins
Chris Tons
Shawn Turney
Paul Tylar

Samuel Tyner
Virginia Valocchi
Jessica Veto
Karen E. Volton
Darlas Von Feldt
Patricia Walton
Robert Warren III
Chris Weber
Kristen Wehrli
Dave B. Weigand
Neil Weigert
Richart T. Weldon
Dale White
Marilyn White
Deanna Williams
Catherine Wilson
Michael Wisneski
Jacqueline Wisniewski
Lynda Woodhall
Wendy Woodhall
Kevin Wright
John S. Yanz
Ivy Yau
Mark Young
Robert Young
Billy F. Zamora
Anna M. Zemko
Monica Zorens
Jun Xia

Chronological List of Buildings, Projects and Credits

1980

Crystal Center
Design 1980
Denver, Colorado
Chesman Realty Company
Principal in charge of design: Curtis W. Fentress
Design team: Brian Chaffee, Lisa K. Fudge
Building type: Retail
Structure: Steel frame
Exterior finish: Granite, glass
Interior finish: Glass, granite, carpet
Gross square feet: 1,000,000
Number of floors: 5
Parking: 2,000 spaces

One Mile High Plaza
Design 1980
Denver, Colorado
J. Roulier Interests
Principal in charge of design: Curtis W. Fentress
Design team: Brian Chaffee, Mary Jane Donovan, Lisa K. Fudge, Chris Weber
Building type: Office
Structure: Steel frame, concrete core
Exterior finish: Granite, glass
Interior finish: Granite, glass, gypsum board, carpet
Gross square feet: 947,000
Number of floors: 37
Parking: 1,000 spaces

Terrace Towers Master Plan
Design 1980–86
Engelwood, Colorado
J. Roulier Interests
Principal in charge of design: Curtis W. Fentress
Principal in charge of production: James H. Bradburn
Design team: Robert Busch, Brian Chaffee, Gregory R. Gidez, Stuart A. Schunck, Dave B. Weigand
Building type: Mixed-use (office, retail, hotel, parking)
Structure: Steel frame, concrete core
Exterior finish: Limestone, glass
Gross square feet: 7,000,000
Number of floors: 4–36
Parking: 12,000 spaces
Site: 48 acres

Terrace Building
Design/Completion 1980/1981
Englewood, Colorado
J. Roulier Interests
Principal in charge of design: Curtis W. Fentress
Design team: Robert T. Brodie, Brian Chaffee, Mary Jane Donovan, Lisa K. Fudge, Frederic M. Harrington
Building type: Office, parking
Structure: Precast concrete
Exterior finish: Glass, architectural precast concrete
Interior finish: Architectural precast concrete, wood, brick, carpet, glass
Gross square feet: 120,000
Number of floors: 3
Parking: 400 spaces

Southbridge One
Design/Completion 1980/1981
Littleton, Colorado
J. Roulier Interests
Principal in charge of design: Curtis W. Fentress

Design team: Robert Brodie, Lisa K. Fudge, Elizabeth Hamilton, Frederic M. Harrington, Robert J. O'Donnell
Building type: Office
Structure: Precast concrete
Exterior finish: Brick, glass
Interior finish: Brick, wood, glass, carpet, gypsum board
Gross square feet: 70,000 (office)
Number of floors: 2
Parking: 200 spaces

Milestone Tower Headquarters
Design/Completion 1980/1982
Englewood, Colorado
J. Roulier Interests
Principal in charge of design: Curtis W. Fentress
Principal in charge of production: James H. Bradburn
Design team: Benjamin Berg, Donald W. DeCoster, Mary Jane Donovan, Robert C. Grubbs, John L. Mason
Building type: Office
Structure: Steel frame, concrete core
Exterior finish: Limestone, glass
Interior finish: Limestone, granite, carpet, glass
Gross square feet: 240,000 (office)
Number of floors: 12
Parking: 1,000 spaces

Kittredge Building
Design/Completion 1980/1981
Denver, Colorado
Kittredge Properties
Principal in charge of design: Curtis W. Fentress
Principal in charge of production: James H. Bradburn
Design team: Deborah R. Allen, Brian Chaffee, Peter Frothingham, Gregory R. Gidez, Frederic M. Harrington, James F. Hartman, JoAnne Hege, Patrick M. McKelvey, Robert J. O'Donnell, John R. Taylor
Building type: Office renovation
Structure: Steel frame, cast iron, wood
Exterior finish: Rhyolite, brick, glass
Interior finish: Gypsum board, oak, granite, glass, carpet
Gross square feet: 102,000
Number of floors: 8

1981

116 Inverness Drive East
Design/Completion 1981/1982
Englewood, Colorado
Central Development Group
Principal in charge of design: Curtis W. Fentress
Principal in charge of production: James H. Bradburn
Design team: Gregory R. Gidez, James F. Hartman, Michael Kicklighter, Dan Naegele, James Niemi, Byron Stewart
Building type: Office
Structure: Steel frame, concrete core
Exterior finish: Glass
Interior finish: Slate, stainless steel, gypsum board, carpet
Gross square feet: 230,000 (office)
Number of floors: 4
Parking: 1,000 spaces

1999 Broadway
Design/Completion 1981/1985
Denver, Colorado
First Interstate Structures Inc.
Principal in charge of design: Curtis W. Fentress
Principal in charge of production: James H. Bradburn
Project designer: Michael O. Winters
Project manager: John K. McCauley
Job captain: Brit Probst
Design team: Robert T. Brodie, Robert G. Datson, Donald W. DeCoster, Lawrence Depenbusch, Douglas Dick, Gregory R. Gidez, Frederic M. Harrington, Michael Kicklighter, John M. Kudrycki, John L. Mason, Patrick M. McKelvey, James Niemi, Clement Okoye, Frederick R. Pax, Sandy Prouty, John R. Taylor, Toshika Yoshida
Building type: Office
Structure: Steel frame, concrete core
Exterior finish: Post-tensioned limestone, glass, stainless steel
Interior finish: Marble, granite, stainless steel, gypsum board, carpet
Gross square feet: 760,000
Number of floors: 43
Parking: 1,000 spaces

Holy Ghost Roman Catholic Church
Design/Completion 1981/1985
Denver, Colorado
Lawder Corporation
Principal in charge of design: Curtis W. Fentress
Principal in charge of production: James H. Bradburn
Project architect: Michael O. Winters
Project manager: John L. Mason
Design team: Elizabeth Hamilton, John M. Kudrycki, Patrick M. McKelvey, Bruce R. Mosteller, John R. Taylor
Building type: Church renovation/restoration
Structure: Concrete, steel, brick
Exterior finish: Terra cotta tiles, brick
Interior finish: Gypsum board, brick, marble, wood
Gross square feet: 28,000
Number of floors: 3

1982

Reliance Tower
Design 1982
Denver, Colorado
Reliance Development
Principal in charge of design: Curtis W. Fentress
Principal in charge of production: James H. Bradburn
Design team: Robert T. Brodie, Brian Chaffee, Gary Chamer, Lisa K. Fudge, Gregory R. Gidez, JoAnne Hege, John K. McCauley, Patrick M. McKelvey, James Niemi, Michael O. Winters
Building type: Office, retail, parking
Structure: Steel frame, concrete core
Exterior finish: Granite, glass
Interior finish: Granite, glass, gypsum board, carpet
Gross square feet: 1,400,000
Number of floors: 57
Parking: 2,000 spaces

Capitol Tower/J.D. Tower
Design 1982
Denver, Colorado
Dikeou Family Interest

Principal in charge of design: Curtis W. Fentress
Design team: Gary Chamer
Building type: Office
Structure: Steel frame
Exterior finish: Granite, glass
Interior finish: Granite, glass, gypsum board, carpet
Gross square feet: 1,186,000
Number of floors: 50
Parking: 1,000 spaces

Odd Fellows Hall
Design/Completion 1982/1983
Denver, Colorado
Cambridge Development Group
Principal in charge of design: Curtis W. Fentress
Principal in charge of production: James H. Bradburn
Design team: Deborah R. Allen, Frederic M. Harrington, James F. Hartman, JoAnne Hege, Leslie Leydorf, Carla McConnell, Patrick M. McKelvey, James Niemi, Nathaniel A. Taiwo, Dave B. Weigand, Richard T. Weldon, Toshika Yoshida
Building type: Adaptive reuse of office building
Structure: Brick, cast iron, wood, steel
Exterior finish: Sandstone, brick, painted metal
Interior finish: Gypsum board, tiles, carpet, glass
Gross square feet: 32,700
Number of floors: 5

Museum of Western Art/The Navarre
Design/Completion 1982/1983
Denver, Colorado
William Foxley
Principal in charge of design: Curtis W. Fentress
Principal in charge of production: James H. Bradburn
Associate architect: John Prosser
Design team: Deborah R. Allen, Donald W. DeCoster, Douglas Dick
Building type: Museum
Structure: Wood frame
Exterior finish: Brick, painted millwork
Interior finish: Gypsum board, tiles, carpet
Gross square feet: 20,000
Number of floors: 5

Southbridge Plaza
Design/Completion 1982/1984
Littleton, Colorado
Southbridge Plaza Association Inc.
Principal in charge of design: Curtis W. Fentress
Principal in charge of production: James H. Bradburn
Design team: Elizabeth Hamilton, Kimble Hobbs, Bruce R. Mosteller, W. Harrison Phillips, Brit Probst, Bryon Stewart
Building type: Retail
Structure: Light steel, masonry
Exterior finish: Brick, cedar
Interior finish: Gypsum board, aluminum
Gross square feet: 182,500
Number of floors: 1
Parking: 800 spaces

Welton Street Parking Garage
Design/Completion 1982/1985
Denver, Colorado
Lawder Corporation
Principal in charge of design: Curtis W. Fentress
Principal in charge of production: James H. Bradburn

Project architect: Michael O. Winters
Project manager: John K. McCauley
Job captain: Patrick M. McKelvey
Design team: Douglas Dick, Frederic M. Harrington, Kimble Hobbs, John L. Mason, Brit Probst
Building type: Parking
Structure: Precast concrete
Exterior finish: Architectural precast concrete, glass
Interior finish: Concrete
Gross square feet: 205,000
Number of floors: 9
Parking: 1,000 spaces

1800 Grant Street
Design/Completion 1982/1985
Denver, Colorado
1800 Grant Street Association Ltd
Principal in charge of design: Curtis W. Fentress
Principal in charge of production: James H. Bradburn
Project designer: Brian Chaffee
Project manager: John K. McCauley
Job captain: James F. Hartman
Design team: Deborah R. Allen, Gregory R. Gidez, Renata Hajek, JoAnne Hege, Mark A. Wagner, Toshika Yoshida
Building type: Office
Structure: Steel frame, concrete core
Exterior finish: Granite, glass
Interior finish: Granite, glass block, gypsum board
Gross square feet: 121,000
Number of floors: 8
Parking: 400 spaces

1983

YMCA
Design 1983
Denver, Colorado
Jeffrey Selby & Jay Peterson, Associates
Principal in charge of design: Curtis W. Fentress
Principal in charge of production: James H. Bradburn
Design team: Gary Chamer
Building type: Office, YMCA, parking
Structure: Steel frame, concrete core
Exterior finish: Architectural precast concrete, granite
Interior finish: Granite, glass, gypsum board, carpet
Gross square feet: 1,154,000
Number of floors: 55
Parking: 500 spaces

Temple Sinai
Design/Completion 1983/1984
Denver, Colorado
Temple Sinai Congregation
Principal in charge of design: Curtis W. Fentress
Principal in charge of production: James H. Bradburn
Project designer: B. Edward Balkin
Project manager: John K. McCauley
Design team: Ava Dahlstrom, Dalas Disney, John R. Taylor
Building type: Synagogue
Structure: Steel frame, precast concrete
Exterior finish: Brick, glass
Interior finish: Carpet, gypsum board, wood
Gross square feet: 22,500
Number of floors: 1
Parking: 300 spaces

Balboa Company Corporate Headquarters
Design/Completion 1983/1984
Denver, Colorado
Captiva Corporation
Principal in charge of design: Curtis W. Fentress
Principal in charge of production: James H. Bradburn
Design team: Deborah R. Allen, Donald W. DeCoster, Gregory R. Gidez, JoAnne Hege, Stan Kulesa, James W. O'Neill, Toshika Yoshida
Building type: Interior design
Interior finish: Marble, mahogany, glass, carpet
Gross square feet: 10,000
Number of floors: 1

Republic Park Hotel
Design/Completion 1983/1985
Englewood, Colorado
Stan Miles Properties
Principal in charge of design: Curtis W. Fentress
Principal in charge of production: James H. Bradburn
Project manager: Mark A. Wagner
Interior designer: Victor Huff and Associates
Design team: Lyle R. Anderson, Brian Chaffee, Gary Chamer, John K. McCauley
Building type: Hotel
Structure: Post-tensioned concrete
Exterior finish: Brick, tinted glass
Interior finish: Gypsum board, vinyl wall covering, wood, carpet
Gross square feet: 169,000
Number of floors: 10
Parking: 250 spaces

One DTC
Design/Completion 1983/1985
Englewood, Colorado
Murray Properties of Colorado
Principal in charge of design: Curtis W. Fentress
Principal in charge of production: James H. Bradburn
Project designer: B. Edward Balkin
Project manager: Dalas Disney
Design team: Deborah R. Allen, Lyle R. Anderson, Garrett H. Christnacht, Gregory R. Gidez, Renata Hajek, Frederic M. Harrington, Stan Kulesa, James Niemi, Clement Okoye, Brit Probst, John R.Taylor, Toshika Yoshida
Building type: Office, parking
Structure (office): Steel frame, concrete core, precast concrete, composite
Structure (parking): Precast concrete
Exterior finish (office): Granite, glass, stainless steel
Exterior finish (parking): Architectural precast concrete
Interior finish (office): Granite, mahogany, carpet, glass
Gross square feet: 230,000
Number of floors: 15
Parking: 1,000 spaces

Tele-Communications Inc. Headquarters
Terrace Tower II
Design/Completion 1983/1985
Englewood, Colorado
J. Roulier Interests, Developer
First Texas Savings Association
Principal in charge of design: Curtis W. Fentress
Principal in charge of production: James H. Bradburn

Project designer: Michael O. Winters
Design team: Deborah R. Allen, Donald W. DeCoster, Frank G. Hege, John M. Kudrycki, James Niemi, Frederick R. Pax, Brit Probst
Building type: Office, parking
Structure (tower): Steel frame, concrete core
Structure (parking): Precast concrete
Exterior finish: Limestone, granite
Interior finish: Limestone, granite, carpet, gypsum board, glass
Gross square feet: 240,000
Number of floors: 12
Parking: 1,000 spaces

1984

Englewood Mixed-Use Center
Design 1984
Englewood, Colorado
Talley Corporation
Principal in charge of design: Curtis W. Fentress
Principal in charge of production: James H. Bradburn
Design team: B. Edward Balkin, Douglas Dick
Building type: Office, retail, apartments, hotel, health club
Structure: Steel frame, precast concrete
Exterior finish: Glass, architectural precast concrete
Gross square feet: 1,800,000
Number of floors: 2–12
Parking: 6,000 spaces
Site: 40 acres

Tucson City Center Master Plan
Design 1984
Tucson, Arizona
Reliance Development Group
Principal in charge of design: Curtis W. Fentress
Principal in charge of production: James H. Bradburn
Design team: Michael O. Winters
Building type: Office, retail, hotel, parking
Structure: Steel frame, concrete core
Exterior finish: Granite, glass
Interior finish: Granite, glass, gypsum board, carpet
Gross square feet: 725,000
Number of floors: 30
Parking: 700 spaces

Castlewood Plaza Master Plan
Design 1984
Englewood, Colorado
J. Roulier Interests
Principal in charge of design: Curtis W. Fentress
Principal in charge of production: James H. Bradburn
Design team: B. Edward Balkin, Steve Nelson
Building type: Mixed-use master plan (office, hotel, retail)
Structure: Precast concrete
Exterior finish: Architectural precast concrete
Interior finish: Wood, glass, gypsum board, carpet
Gross square feet: 3,000,000
Parking: 9,000 spaces

Mountain Bell Special Services Center
Design 1984
Denver, Colorado
Mountain Bell
Principal in charge of design: Curtis W. Fentress
Principal in charge of production: James H. Bradburn

Design team: Deborah R. Allen, Donald W. DeCoster, Annette English, Gregory R. Gidez, Frank G. Hege, JoAnne Hege, James W. O'Neill, Frederick R. Pax, Toshika Yoshida
Building type: Interior design
Interior finish: Gypsum board, fabric, carpet, wood
Gross square feet: 46,000 (office)
Number of floors: 1

Pioneer Plaza Hotel
Design 1984
Denver, Colorado
Cambridge Development Group
Principal in charge of design: Curtis W. Fentress
Principal in charge of production: James H. Bradburn
Design team: Gary Chamer, Lisa K. Fudge, Gregory R. Gidez, Michael O. Winters
Building type: Hotel, office, retail, parking
Structure: Steel frame, concrete core
Exterior finish: Granite, glass
Interior finish: Granite, glass, gypsum board, carpet, wood
Gross square feet: 1,097,437
Number of floors: 24
Parking: 1,000 spaces

Greenville Park Tower
Design 1984
Dallas, Texas
JRI International/Robert Halloway Corporation
Principal in charge of design: Curtis W. Fentress
Principal in charge of production: James H. Bradburn
Project architect: Michael O. Winters
Design team: Garrett M. Christnacht, Steven O. Gregory, Clement Okoye, James W. O'Neill, John R. Taylor
Building type: Office
Structure: Steel frame, concrete core
Exterior finish: Glass, metal
Interior finish: Marble, stainless steel, gypsum board, carpet
Gross square feet: 296,889
Number of floors: 15
Parking: 1,000 spaces

Lexington Center
Design/Completion 1984/1985
Colorado Springs, Colorado
Techkor Development
Principal in charge of design: Curtis W. Fentress
Principal in charge of production: James H. Bradburn
Project designer: Brian Chaffee
Project manager: John K. McCauley
Job captain: Patrick M. McKelvey
Building type: Office, research
Structure: Steel frame
Exterior finish: Concrete masonry units, metal panel
Interior finish: Concrete masonry units
Gross square feet: 78,200
Number of floors: 2
Parking: 150 spaces

Norwest Tower
Design/Completion 1984/1986
Tucson, Arizona
Reliance Development Group
Principal in charge of design: Curtis W. Fentress
Principal in charge of production: James H. Bradburn

Project designer: Michael O. Winters
Project manager: Stan Kulesa
Design team: Jane Bertschinger, Brian Chaffee, Garrett M. Christnacht, Douglas Dick, Donald W. DeCoster, Gregory R. Gidez, Frank G. Hege, Renata Hajek, John L. Mason, James Niemi, James W. O'Neill, Jim Snyder
Building type: Office
Structure: Steel frame, concrete core
Exterior finish: Granite, glass
Interior finish: Granite, bronze, carpet, wood, glass, gypsum board, painted aluminium
Gross square feet: 500,000
Number of floors: 23
Parking: 500 spaces

Data General Field Engineering Logistics Center
Design/Completion 1984/1986
Fountain, Colorado
Data General Corporation
Principal in charge of design: Curtis W. Fentress
Principal in charge of production: James H. Bradburn
Project designer: B. Edward Balkin
Job Captain: John M. Kudrycki
Project manager: Brit Probst
Design team: Garrett M. Christnacht, Frank G. Hege, Renata Hajek, Steven Fritzky
Building type: Manufacturing
Structure: Steel frame
Exterior finish: Architectural precast concrete, glass
Interior finish: Gypsum board, carpet, tiles
Gross square feet: 320,000
Number of floors: 2
Parking: 1,000 spaces

1985

Centennial Office Park Master Plan
Design 1985
Englewood, Colorado
Mission Viejo
Principal in charge of design: Curtis W. Fentress
Principal in charge of production: James H. Bradburn
Design team: B. Edward Balkin, Charlotte C. Breed
Building type: Master plan for mixed-use development
Structure: Steel frame, concrete
Exterior finish: Brick, glass
Interior finish: Gypsum board, carpet, glass
Gross square feet: 906,550
Number of floors: 2–6
Parking: 3,000 spaces

Parkway Plaza Master Plan
Design 1985
Littleton, Colorado
Talley Corporation
Principal in charge of design: Curtis W. Fentress
Principal in charge of production: James H. Bradburn
Design team: Charlotte C. Breed
Building type: Master plan (office park, retail, hotel)
Structure: Precast concrete
Exterior finish: Architectural precast concrete, brick, glass
Interior finish: Gypsum board, glass, carpet
Gross square feet: 6,674,000
Parking: 18,000 spaces

Fiddler's Green Amphitheater
Design 1985
Englewood, Colorado
John Madden Company
Principal in charge of design: Curtis W. Fentress
Principal in charge of production: James H. Bradburn
Design team: Amy Solomon, Galen Bailey, Todd R. Britton
Building type: Amphitheater
Structure: Steel frame, fabric
Exterior finish: Fiberglass, architectural precast concrete
Interior finish: Fabric, concrete
Gross square feet: 100,000
Number of floors: 1

1986

Black American West Museum
Design/Completion 1986/1987
Denver, Colorado
Black American West Museum
Principal in charge of design: Curtis W. Fentress
Principal in charge of production: James H. Bradburn
Project architect: James F. Hartman
Design team: Mark Brinkman, Donald W. DeCoster, Mary Jane Koenig, Francis Mishler
Building type: Museum
Structure: Brick, wood
Exterior finish: Brick, glass, wood
Interior finish: Gypsum board, plaster, wood, carpet
Gross square feet: 2,700
Number of floors: 3

Idaho Power Company Corporate Headquarters
Design/Completion 1986/1989
Boise, Idaho
Idaho Power Company
Principal in charge of design: Curtis W. Fentress
Principal in charge of production: James H. Bradburn
Architect of record: CSHQA Associates
Project architect: Michael O. Winters
Space planning: Sandy Prouty
Design team: Robert G. Datson, Karin Mason, Jack M. Mousseau, Jun Xia
Building type: Office
Structure: Steel frame, concrete core
Exterior finish: Etched and honed glass fiber reinforced concrete, granite, glass
Interior finish: Travertine, granite, bronze, carpet, gypsum board
Gross square feet: 217,000
Number of floors: 9 (plus 1 sub-floor)
Parking: 900 spaces

Jefferson County Human Services Building
Design/Completion 1986/1989
Golden, Colorado
Jefferson County, Colorado
Principal in charge of design: Curtis W. Fentress
Principal in charge of production: James H. Bradburn
Design team: B. Edward Balkin, Renata Hajek, Barbara K. Hochstetler, John M. Kudrycki, John L. Mason, Mark A. Wagner
Building type: Office
Structure: Steel frame, concrete core
Exterior finish: Brick, glass

Interior finish: Drywall
Gross square feet: 165,000
Number of floors: 4
Parking: 1,000 spaces

Colorado School of Mines
Design/Completion 1986/1990
Golden, Colorado
Colorado School of Mines
Principal in charge of design: Curtis W. Fentress
Principal in charge of production: James H. Bradburn
Design team: Robert G. Datson, James F. Hartman, Nancy Kettner, Ned Kirschbaum, Robert Root, Robert Young
Building type: Classrooms, research
Structure: Masonry, wood, steel
Exterior finish: Masonry
Interior finish: Gypsum board, carpet
Gross square feet: 14,000
Number of floors: 3

Ronstadt Transit Center
Design/Completion 1986/1991
Tucson, Arizona
City of Tucson
Principal in charge of design: Curtis W. Fentress
Principal in charge of production: James H. Bradburn
Project designer: Brian Chaffee
Project manager: Robert Louden,
Design team: James Carpenter, John L. Mason, Clement Okoye, Robert Root, Michael O. Winters
Building type: Public transit station
Structure: Steel frame
Exterior finish: Brick, painted steel
Interior finish: Concrete block, tiles
Gross square feet: 95,832
Number of floors: 1

Jefferson County Government Center Master Plan
Design/Completion 1986/1989–92
Golden, Colorado
Jefferson County, Colorado
Principal in charge of design: Curtis W. Fentress
Principal in charge of production: James H. Bradburn
Project architect: B. Edward Balkin
Design team: Brian Chaffee
Building type: Master plan
Structure: Steel frame, concrete
Exterior: Masonry, architectural precast concrete, glass
Gross square feet: 1,000,000
Parking: 2,000 spaces
Site: 180 acres

1987

Sun Plaza
Design 1987
Colorado Springs, Colorado
Sun Resources Inc.
Principal in charge of design: Curtis W. Fentress
Principal in charge of production: James H. Bradburn
Project designer: Luis O. Acosta
Project manager: John K. McCauley
Job captain: Patrick M. McKelvey
Design team: Sandy Brand, Gregory R. Gidez, Frederick R. Pax, John R. Taylor
Building type: Office

Structure: Steel frame
Exterior finish: Granite, glass
Interior finish: Granite, glass, gypsum board, carpet
Gross square feet: 310,000
Number of floors: 24
Parking: 1,000 spaces

Boise Civic Center
Design 1987
Boise, Idaho
Dick Holtz
Principal in charge of design: Curtis W. Fentress
Principal in charge of production: James H. Bradburn
Project architect: Michael O. Winters
Project type: Redevelopment plan for 30-block downtown area
Building type: Office, hotel, retail, parking
Structure: Steel frame, concrete
Exterior finish: Glass, architectural precast concrete, masonry
Gross square feet: 2,000,000
Number of floors: 2–24
Parking: 6,000 spaces
Site: 30 blocks

Colorado Convention Center
Design/Completion 1987/1990
Denver, Colorado
City and County of Denver
Principal in charge of design: Curtis W. Fentress
Principal in charge of production: James H. Bradburn
Associate architects: Loschky MarQuardt and Nesholm; Bertram A. Bruton and Associates
Project designer: Michael O. Winters
Project manager: Brit Probst
Interior designer: Barbara K. Hochstetler
Design team: B. Edward Balkin, Ronald R. Booth, Richard Burkett, Brian Chaffee, Melanie Colcord, Gregory R. Gidez, Nancy Kettner, John M. Kudrycki, Lauren Lee, Greg Lemon, Beverly G. Pax, John M. Salisbury, Les Stuart, Mark A. Wagner
Building type: Conference center, exhibition hall
Structure: Steel frame, precast concrete
Exterior finish: Architectural precast concrete, glass, concrete masonry units
Interior finish: Concrete, gypsum board, concrete masonry units, terrazzo, carpet
Gross square feet: 1,000,000
Number of floors: 3

1988

Oxbridge Town Center
Design 1988
Oxbridge, England
David Sparrow
Principal in charge of design: Curtis W. Fentress
Principal in charge of production: James H. Bradburn
Project designer: Michael O. Winters
Design team: Douglas Dick
Building type: Office
Structure: Steel frame, composite concrete
Exterior finish: Glass, metal, granite
Interior finish: Granite
Gross square feet: 176,000
Number of floors: 12
Parking: 400 spaces

Denver Permit Center
Design/Completion 1988/1989
Denver, Colorado
City and County of Denver, Colorado
Principal in charge of design: Curtis W. Fentress
Principal in charge of production: James H.
Bradburn
Design team: James Carpenter, Robert G. Datson,
Philip Davis, James F. Hartman, Beverly G. Pax,
Frederick R. Pax, Robert Root, John M. Salisbury,
Les Stuart
Building type: Office
Structure: Steel frame, concrete
Exterior finish: Brick, synthetic stucco
Interior finish: Brick, tiles, gypsum board, carpet
Gross square feet: 80,000
Number of floors: 4
Parking: 20 spaces

Franklin and Lake
Design/Completion 1988/1989
Chicago, Illinois
Zeller Realty
Principal in charge of design: Curtis W. Fentress
Principal in charge of production: James H.
Bradburn
Project architect: Michael O. Winters
Design team: Jun Xia
Building type: Parking, retail
Structure: Post-tensioned concrete
Exterior finish: Architectural precast concrete, glass,
painted metal
Gross square feet: 387,000
Number of floors: 13
Parking: 1,300 spaces

Cherry Creek Plaza
Design/Completion 1988/1990
Denver, Colorado
Bramalea
Principal in charge of design: Curtis W. Fentress
Principal in charge of production: James H.
Bradburn
Design team: B. Edward Balkin
Building type: Office, retail, parking
Structure: Steel frame, concrete core
Exterior finish: Brick, glass
Interior finish: Drywall, carpet
Gross square feet: 800
Number of floors: 8
Parking: 2,000 spaces
Site: 20 acres

**Jefferson County Government Center Courts and
Administration Building**
Design/Completion 1988/1993
Golden, Colorado
Jefferson County, Colorado
Principal in charge of design: Curtis W. Fentress
Principal in charge of production: James H.
Bradburn
Project designer: Brian Chaffee
Project manager: James F. Hartman
Interior designer: Barbara K. Hochstetler
Design team: Gregory D. Billingham, Bill Bramblett,
Sandy J. Brand, Richard Burkett, James Carney,
James Carpenter, Gregory R. Gidez, Ala F. Hason,
Judith Jump, Ned Kirschbaum, Lauren Lee, Robert
Louden, John L. Mason, Clement Okoye, Beverly G.
Pax, Brit Probst, Samuel Tyner, Mark A. Wagner, Lyn
Wisecarver Johnson

Building type: Office, courthouse
Structure: Steel frame, concrete core
Exterior finish: Architectural precast concrete, glass
Interior finish: Wood, architectural precast concrete,
terrazzo, carpet, gypsum board
Gross square feet: 531,000
Number of floors: 7
Parking: 1,200 spaces

1989

**Western and American Galleries, Denver Art
Museum**
Design/Completion 1989
Denver, Colorado
Denver Art Museum
Principal in charge of design: Curtis W. Fentress
Principal in charge of production: James H.
Bradburn
Project manager: Michael Gengler, Robert Root,
John M. Salisbury
Building type: Interior design, museum renovation
Structure: Steel frame, concrete
Interior finish: Gypsum board, fabric, carpet, wood
Gross square feet: 14,000
Number of floors: 1

Estes Park Community and Conference Center
Design/Completion 1989/1991
Estes Park, Colorado
Town of Estes Park, Colorado
Principal in charge of design: Curtis W. Fentress
Principal in charge of production: James H.
Bradburn
Architect of record: Thorpe and Associates
Principal in charge: Roger Thorpe
Project architect: Christopher A. Carvell
Project manager: Mark A. Wagner
Interior designer: Barbara K. Hochstetler
Building type: Conference center
Structure: Steel frame
Exterior finish: Brick, sandstone, copper,
architectural precast concrete
Interior finish: Lodge pole pine, stone, vinyl wall
covering, carpet
Gross square feet: 65,000
Number of floors: 2

**University of Colorado Mathematics Building and
Gemmill Engineering Sciences Library**
Design/Completion 1989/1992
Boulder, Colorado
University of Colorado
Principal in charge of design: Curtis W. Fentress
Principal in charge of production: James H.
Bradburn
Project designer: Christopher A. Carvell
Project architect: Robert Louden
Interior designer: Gary Morris
Project manager: Nancy Kettner
Design team: Douglas Eichelberger, Greg Lemon,
Michael O. Winters, Jun Xia
Building type: Classrooms, library, research
laboratories
Structure: Steel frame, precast concrete
Exterior finish: Sandstone, architectural precast
concrete
Interior finish: Sandstone, gypsum board, carpet
Gross square feet: 54,500
Number of floors: 4

**Natural Resources Laboratory and Administration
Building**
Design/Completion 1989/1992
Olympia, Washington
State of Washington, General Services
Administration
Principal in charge of design: Curtis W. Fentress
Principal in charge of production: James H.
Bradburn
Project architect: Ronald R. Booth
Interior designer: Barbara K. Hochstetler
Project manager: John M. Kudrycki
Job captain: Gregory R. Gidez
Design team: James Carney, Milan Hart, Arthur A.
Hoy III, Lyn Wisecarver Johnson, Lauren Lee, David
Tompkins, Michael Wisneski
Building type: Office, laboratory
Structure: Steel frame, concrete core
Exterior finish: Architectural precast concrete
Interior finish: Stone, terrazzo, wood
Gross square feet: 325,000
Number of floors: 6 (plus 3 levels of parking)
Parking: 1,200 spaces

Colorado State Capitol Life-Safety Project
Design/Completion 1989/1999
Denver, Colorado
State of Colorado
Principal in charge of design: Curtis W. Fentress
Principal in charge of production: James H.
Bradburn
Project architect: James F. Hartman
Design team: Garrett M Christnacht, Ala F. Hason,
Brian Ostler, John M. Salisbury, Samuel Tyner
Building type: Office renovation/restoration
Structure: Granite, cast-iron columns, wrought-iron
beams, brick arches, concrete fill
Exterior finish: Granite
Interior finish: Marble, plaster, bronze, pine
Gross square feet: 250,000
Number of floors: 7

1990

Westlake Residences
Design 1990
Seattle, Washington
Astral Investments
Principal in charge of design: Curtis W. Fentress
Principal in charge of production: James H.
Bradburn
Project architect: Christopher A. Carvell
Project manager: Mark A. Wagner
Design team: Richard Burkett, Peter D. Carlson
Building type: Apartments, retail, parking, health
club, pool
Structure: Moment frame, post-tensioned concrete
frame
Exterior finish: Architectural precast concrete, glass
Interior finish: Carpet, drywall
Gross square feet: 450,000
Number of floors: 32
Size: 450 units
Parking: 200 spaces
Site: 20,000 square feet

809 Olive Way
Design 1990
Seattle, Washington
Western Securities Ltd

Principal in charge of design: Curtis W. Fentress
Principal in charge of production: James H.
Bradburn
Project architect: Christopher A. Carvell
Project manager: Mark A. Wagner
Design team: Ronald R. Booth, Robert Louden
Building type: Apartments, retail, parking, health
club, pool
Structure: Concrete, moment frame
Exterior finish: Brick, glass
Interior finish: Carpet, drywall
Gross square feet: 400,000
Number of floors: 24
Size: 400 living units
Parking: 400 spaces
Site: 20,000 square feet

Denver Central Library and Urban Analysis
Design 1990
Denver, Colorado
City and County of Denver, Colorado
Principal in charge of design: Curtis W. Fentress
Principal in charge of production: James H.
Bradburn
Design team: Arthur A. Hoy III, Michel Pariseau
Building type: Library, storage
Structure: Concrete
Exterior finish: Stone, glass
Interior finish: Drywall, carpet
Gross square feet: 500,000
Number of floors: 6
Site: 100,000 square feet

Union Station Redevelopment Plan
Design 1990–91
Denver, Colorado
Union Station Redevelopment Committee
Principal in charge of design: Curtis W. Fentress
Principal in charge of production: James H.
Bradburn
Design team: Galen Bailey, Todd R. Britton, Arthur
A. Hoy III
Building type: Mixed-use (office, retail, apartments,
hotel, museum, parking)
Structure: Steel frame, concrete core
Exterior finish: Architectural precast concrete, brick,
glass
Interior finish: Carpet, drywall
Gross square feet: 3,000,000
Number of floors: 4–30
Parking: 8,000 spaces
Site: 40 acres

IBM Customer Service Center
Design/Completion 1990/1992
Denver, Colorado
IBM
Principal in charge of design: Curtis W. Fentress
Principal in charge of production: James H.
Bradburn
Project designer: Barbara K. Hochstetler
Project manager: Donald W. DeCoster
Design team: Robert G. Datson, Kathleen Corner
Galvin, John A. Gossett, Judith Jump, Sandy Prouty,
Michael O. Winters
Building type: Interior design
Interior finish: Gypsum board, fabric, carpet
Gross square feet: 100,000
Number of floors: 4

1991

Cathedral Square
Design 1991
Milwaukee, Wisconsin
Corum Real Estate Group
Principal in charge of design: Curtis W. Fentress
Principal in charge of production: James H.
Bradburn
Design team: Peter D. Carlson
Building type: Mixed-use (apartments, retail,
parking, health club, pool)
Structure: Concrete
Exterior finish: Brick, glass
Interior finish: Carpet, drywall
Gross square feet: 500,000
Number of floors: 27
Parking: 600 spaces
Site: 40,000 square feet

University Art Museum, University of California at Santa Barbara
Design 1991
Santa Barbara, California
University of California at Santa Barbara
Principal in charge of design: Curtis W. Fentress
Principal in charge of production: James H.
Bradburn
Associate architect: John Prosser
Project architect: Michael O. Winters
Design team: Douglas Dick
Building type: Museum
Structure: Steel frame
Exterior finish: Stucco
Interior finish: Stone, stucco
Gross square feet: 60,000
Number of floors: 3

Denver International Airport Passenger Terminal Complex
Design/Completion 1991/1994
Denver, Colorado
City and County of Denver
Principal in charge of design: Curtis W. Fentress
Principal in charge of production: James H.
Bradburn
Associate architect: Pouw and Associates Inc.;
Bertram A. Bruton and Associates
Project architect: Michael O. Winters
Project manager: Thomas J. Walsh
Interior designer: Barbara K. Hochstetler
Project director: Brit Probst
Job captains: Joseph Solomon, John M. Salisbury
Design team: Galen Bailey, Todd R. Britton, Richard
Burkett, James Carney, James Carpenter, Brian
Chaffee, Garrett M. Christnacht, John Gagnon,
Kathleen Galvin, Michael Gengler, Gregory R. Gidez,
Warren Hogue III, Doris Hung, Charles Johns,
Anthia Kappos, Michael Klebba, John M. Kudrycki,
Lauren Lee, Robert Louden, Michael Miller, Gary
Morris, Jack M. Mousseau, A. Chris Olson, Brian
Ostler, Teri Paris, Frederick R. Pax, Robert Root,
Tim Roush, Amy Solomon, Les Stuart, Dave
Tompkins, Samuel Tyner, Mark A. Wagner, John C.
Wurzenberger Jr, Jun Xia
Building type: Airport
Structure: Steel frame, precast concrete, fabric
structure
Exterior finish: Teflon-coated fiberglass, glass,
architectural precast concrete

Interior finish: Granite, stainless steel, glass
Gross square feet: 2,250,000 (plus 3,500,000 parking)
Number of floors: 6
Parking: 12,000 spaces

National Museum of Wildlife Art
Design/Completion 1991/1995
Jackson, Wyoming
National Museum of Wildlife Art/Bill and Joffa Kerr
Principal in charge of design: Curtis W. Fentress
Principal in charge of production: James H.
Bradburn
Project architect: Brian Chaffee
Interior designer: Barbara Fentress, Gary Morris
Job captain: Gregory R. Gidez
Design team: Anthia Kappos, Brian Ostler, Tim
Roush
Building type: Museum
Structure: Steel frame, concrete
Exterior finish: Stone, glass
Interior finish: Stone, gypsum board, carpet, wood
Gross square feet: 55,453
Number of floors: 2
Parking: 250 spaces

National Cowboy Hall of Fame
Design/Completion 1991/1997
Oklahoma City, Oklahoma
National Cowboy Hall of Fame
Principal in charge of design: Curtis W. Fentress
Principal in charge of production: James H.
Bradburn
Project architect: Ronald R. Booth
Interior designer: Barbara K. Hochstetler
Project manager: Mark A. Wagner
Job captain: Gregory D. Billingham
Design team: Peter D. Carlson, John Gagnon, John
M. McGahey, Gary Morris, Jack M. Mousseau, Teri
Paris, Thomas P. Theobald
Building type: Museum
Structure: Steel frame
Exterior finish: Sandstone
Interior finish: Sandstone, wood, carpet
Gross square feet: 240,000
Number of floors: 2
Parking: 1,000 spaces

1992

Dinosaur Discovery Museum
Design 1992
Canyon City, Colorado
Garden Park Paleontological Society
Principal in charge of design: Curtis W. Fentress
Principal in charge of production: James H.
Bradburn
Project architect: Brian Chaffee
Design team: Carl J. Dalio, Wilbur Moore
Building type: Museum, visitor center
Structure: Steel frame, concrete
Exterior finish: Architectural precast concrete, steel,
glass
Interior finish: Stone, wood, carpet, gypsum board
Gross square feet: 60,000
Number of floors: 4

West Hills Hotel
Design 1992
Keystone, Colorado
Chamer Development
Principal in charge of design: Curtis W. Fentress

Principal in charge of production: James H. Bradburn
Project architect: Michael O. Winters
Project manager: Brit Probst
Design team: Gary Chamer, Mark A. Wagner
Building type: Hotel, conference center
Structure: Steel frame, concrete
Exterior finish: Architectural precast concrete, glass, wrought iron
Interior finish: Stone, wood, carpet, gypsum board
Gross square feet: 260,000
Number of floors: 6
Parking: 500,000 spaces

Eastbank Conference Center and Hotel
Design 1992
Wichita, Kansas
Ross Investment
Principal in charge of design: Curtis W. Fentress
Principal in charge of production: James H. Bradburn
Project architect: Mark A. Wagner
Interior designer: Barbara K. Hochstetler
Building type: Hotel, conference center
Structure: Post-tensioned concrete
Exterior finish: Brick, limestone, glass
Interior finish: Brick, limestone, carpet, wood
Gross square feet: 205,000
Number of floors: 14
Parking: 500 spaces

Colorado Convention Center Hotel
Design 1992
Denver, Colorado
J. Roulier Interests
Principal in charge of design: Curtis W. Fentress
Principal in charge of production: James H. Bradburn
Design team: Galen Bailey, Todd R. Britton, Amy Solomon, Jun Xia
Building type: Hotel, conference rooms, restaurants
Structure: Concrete
Exterior finish: Architectural precast concrete, glass
Interior finish: Carpet, drywall
Gross square feet: 400,000
Number of floors: 30
Rooms: 550 rooms
Parking: 1,000 spaces
Site: 100,000 square feet

Coors Stadium
Design 1992
Denver, Colorado
Denver Metropolitan Major League Baseball Stadium District Commission
Principal in charge of design: Curtis W. Fentress
Principal in charge of production: James H. Bradburn
Associate architect: Ellerbe Becket Inc.
Design team: John A. Gossett, Michael Pariseau
Building type: Baseball stadium
Structure: Steel frame, concrete core
Exterior finish: Brick
Interior finish: Masonry, architectural precast concrete
Gross square feet: 600,000
Number of floors: 32
Capacity: 45,000 seats
Site: 20 acres

Kuala Lumpur Airport
Design 1992
Kuala Lumpur, Malaysia
McClier Aviation Group
Principal in charge of design: Curtis W. Fentress
Principal in charge of production: James H. Bradburn
Design team: Carl J. Dalio, Michael O. Winters
Building type: Airport
Structure: Steel frame, cable
Exterior finish: Glass, fabric roof
Interior finish: Granite, drywall

Moscow Redevelopment Project
Design 1992
Moscow, Russia
Moscow Redevelopment Group
Principal in charge of design: Curtis W. Fentress
Principal in charge of production: James H. Bradburn
Associate architect: Andrei Meerson & Partners
Design team: Arthur A. Hoy III, Jack M. Mousseau, Aleksandr Sheykhet, Michael O. Winters
Building type: Mixed-use (apartments, hotel, office, retail)
Structure: Concrete
Exterior finish: Brick, glass
Interior finish: Brick, glass, carpet, gypsum board
Gross square feet: 5,000,000
Number of floors: 2–30
Parking: 5,000 spaces

Catalina Resort Community
Design 1992
Playa Dantita, Ocotal, Costa Rica
Developments International Inc.
Principal in charge of design: Curtis W. Fentress
Principal in charge of production: James H. Bradburn
Project designer: Barbara K. Hochstetler
Project manager: Jack M. Mousseau
Design team: Wilbur Moore
Building type: Mixed-use resort plan (hotel, marina, retail, recreational, residential)
Hotel: 2,000 rooms
Marina: 500 slips
Shopping center: 100,000 square feet
Residential: 5,000 living units
Structure: Wood frame
Exterior finish: Brick, wood
Interior finish: Brick, stucco, wood, tiles
Gross square feet: 1,500,000
Number of floors: 1–6

Clark County Master Plan
Design 1992
Las Vegas, Nevada
Clark County General Services Department
Principal in charge of design: Curtis W. Fentress
Principal in charge of production: James H. Bradburn
Design team: Arthur A. Hoy III, Michael O. Winters
Gross square feet: 1,655,000

Clark County Government Center
Design/Completion 1992/1995
Las Vegas, Nevada
Clark County General Services Department
Principal in charge of design: Curtis W. Fentress
Principal in charge of production: James H. Bradburn

Associate architect: Domingo Cambeiro Corporation
Project architect: Michael O. Winters
Interior designer: Barbara K. Hochstetler
Project manager: John M. Kudrycki
Job captain: Ned Kirschbaum
Design team: Ronald R. Booth, John A. Gossett, Ala F. Hason, Warren Hogue III, Arthur A. Hoy III, Anthia Kappos, Lauren Lee, Robert Louden, Gary Morris, Joy Spatz, Michael Wisneski, John C. Wurzenberger Jr
Building type: Office
Structure: Steel frame, concrete core
Exterior finish: Sandstone, glass, painted metal
Interior finish: Granite, stucco, carpet, gypsum board
Gross square feet: 375,000
Number of floors: 6 (plus 1 sub-floor)
Parking: 1,200 spaces

National Oceanic and Atmospheric Administration Boulder Research Laboratories
Design/Completion 1992/1998
Boulder, Colorado
United States General Services Administration/ National Oceanic and Atmospheric Administration
Principal in charge of design: Curtis W. Fentress
Principal in charge of production: James H. Bradburn
Project architect: Ronald R. Booth
Interior designer: Barbara K. Hochstetler
Project manager: Jeffrey W. Olson
Design team: Peter D. Carlson, Gregory R. Gidez, Ala F. Hason, Warren Hogue III, Robert Louden, Gary Morris, Teri Paris
Building type: Laboratory
Structure: Cast-in-place concrete
Exterior finish: Architectural precast concrete, stone
Interior finish: Stone, terrazzo
Gross square feet: 371,500
Number of floors: 4

1993

Vladivostok City Center
Design 1993
Vladivostok, Russia
Jupiter Development
Principal in charge of design: Curtis W. Fentress
Principal in charge of production: James H. Bradburn
Project architect: Arthur A. Hoy III
Design team: Doni Mitchell, Aleksandr Sheykhet
Building type: Hotel, office, apartment, parking
Structure: Concrete
Exterior finish: Architectural precast concrete, glass
Interior finish: Carpet, gypsum board
Gross square feet: 1,000,000
Number of floors: 4–30
Parking: 1,000 spaces

Second Bangkok International Airport
Design 1993
Bangkok, Thailand
Airport Authority of Thailand
Principal in charge of design: Curtis W. Fentress
Principal in charge of production: James H. Bradburn
Associate architect: McClier Aviation Group
Project designer: Michael O. Winters
Interior designer: Barbara K. Hochstetler
Project architect: Jack M. Mousseau

Project manager: Thomas J. Walsh
Design team: Galen Bailey, Nina Bazian, Todd R.
Britton, Catherine Dunn, David Goorman, John A.
Gossett, John M. McGahey, Doni Mitchell, Gary
Morris, Minh Nguyen, Brian Ostler, Amy Solomon,
Voraporn Sundarupura
Building type: Airport, train station
Structure: Steel frame, concrete
Exterior finish: Architectural precast concrete, glass,
painted metal
Interior finish: Granite, paint, wood, stainless steel,
architectural precast concrete
Gross square feet: 7,000,000
Number of floors: 6
Parking: 8,000 spaces

Kwangju Bank Headquarters
Design 1993
Kwangju, Republic of Korea
Kwangju Bank
Principal in charge of design: Curtis W. Fentress
Principal in charge of production: James H.
Bradburn
Interior Designer: Barbara Fentress
Design team: Arthur A. Hoy III
Building type: Bank Headquarters, Office
Structure: Steel frame, concrete core
Exterior finish: Glass, stone
Interior finish: Carpet, gypsum board
Gross square feet: 700,000
Number of floors: 35
Parking: 400 spaces

**David Eccles Conference Center and Peery's
Egyptian Theater**
Design/Completion 1993/1996
Ogden, Utah
Weber County, Utah
Principal in charge of design: Curtis W. Fentress
Principal in charge of production: James H.
Bradburn
Architect of record: Sanders Herman Associates
Project designer: Ronald R. Booth
Project architect: Christopher A. Carvell
Project managers: Mark A. Wagner
Design team: Gregory D. Billingham, Peter D.
Carlson, Robert Herman, Michael Sanders, Thomas
P. Theobald
Building type: Conference center, performing arts
complex
Structure: Steel frame on existing masonary
Exterior finish: Brick, terra cotta tiles, limestone
Interior finish: Terra cotta tiles, limestone
Gross square feet: 80,000
Number of floors: 3

**Colorado Christian Home Tennyson Center for
Children and Families**
Design/Completion 1993/1996
Denver, Colorado
National Benevolent Association
Principal in charge of design: Curtis W. Fentress
Principal in charge of production: James H.
Bradburn
Project architect: Arthur A. Hoy III
Technical coordinator: Gregory R. Gidez
Design team: John Gagnon, Warren Hogue III, Terry
Paris
Building type: School
Structure: Steel, concrete block

Exterior: Brick, painted metal, wood, concrete block,
glass
Interior: Tiles, wood, gypsum, concrete block, carpet
Gross square feet: 63,700

Montrose Government Center
Design/Completion 1993/1998
Montrose, Colorado
Montrose County, Colorado
Principal in charge of design: Curtis W. Fentress
Principal in charge of production: James H.
Bradburn
Associate architect: Reilly Johnson, Architects
Project architect: Christopher A. Carvell
Project designer: Brian Chaffee
Design team: Doni Mitchell, Aleksandr Sheykhet
Building type: Courthouse, office, jail
Structure: Steel frame, concrete
Exterior finish: Brick, glass
Interior finish: Marble, gypsum board, carpet
Gross square feet: 110,000
Number of floors: 4
Parking: 200 spaces

**University of Northern Colorado Gunter Hall
Renovation**
Design/Completion 1993/1997
Greeley, Colorado
University of Northern Colorado
Principal in charge of design: Curtis W. Fentress
Principal in charge of production: James H.
Bradburn
Design team: Christopher A. Carvell, John Conklin,
James F. Hartman, Lauren Lee
Building type: Higher education
Structure: Steel
Exterior: Brick, terra cotta, limestone
Interior: Ornamental plaster, vinyl, gypsum, carpet
Gross square feet: 92,000

1994

**The Reconstruction of the Souks of Beirut: An
International Ideas Competition**
Design 1994
Beirut, Lebanon
Solidere
Principal in charge of design: Curtis W. Fentress
Principal in charge of production: James H.
Bradburn
Associate architect: Saudi Diyar Consultants
Project manager: Michael Wisneski
Project architect: Ala F. Hason
Architectural historian: Dr Roger A. Chandler
Researcher: Mark T. Harpe
Design team: Nina Bazian, Jamili Butros Copty,
Barbara Fentress, Yasser R. Kaaki, Jack M. Mousseau,
Minh Nguyen, Voraporn Sundarupura
Building type: Mixed-use (office, retail, apartments,
hotels, museums, restaurants, movie theaters,
mosques, library)
Structure: Steel frame, concrete, masonry
Exterior finish: Stone, plaster, glass
Interior finish: Plaster, stone, ceramic tiles, wood,
carpet
Gross square feet: 1,450,000
Number of floors: 1–6
Parking: 2,850 spaces
Site: 14.83 acres

Hawaii Convention Center
Design 1994
Honolulu, Hawaii
State of Hawaii
Principal in charge of design: Curtis W. Fentress
Principal in charge of production: James H.
Bradburn
Associate architects: DMJM Hawaii; Kauahikaua and
Chun Associates
Project architect: Michael O. Winters
Project manager: John M. Kudrycki
Project designer: Jack M. Mousseau
Interior designer: Gary Morris
Design team: Nina Bazian, Cydney Fisher, Michael
Gengler, Haia Ghalib, John A. Gossett, Ala F. Hason,
John M. McGahey, Aleksandr Sheykhet, Voraporn
Sundarupura, Thomas J. Walsh, John C.
Wurzenburger Jr
Building type: Convention center, exhibition hall
Structure: Steel frame, precast concrete
Exterior finish: Architectural precast concrete, stone
Interior finish: Architectural precast concrete,
gypsum board, concrete masonry units, terrazzo,
carpet
Gross square feet: 1,300,000
Number of floors: 3
Parking: 900 spaces

One Polo Creek
Design/Completion 1994/1997
Denver, Colorado
BCORP Holdings and AIMCO
Principal in charge of design: Curtis W. Fentress
Principal in charge of production: James H.
Bradburn
Project designer: Christopher A. Carvell
Project architects: Robert Louden, John C.
Wurzenburger Jr
Design team: Gregory D. Billingham, Richard
Burkett, William B. Buyers, Peter D. Carlson, Garrett
M. Christnacht, Jayne Coburn, Marc Dietrick,
Catherine Dunn, Jane Hiley, Warren Hogue III,
Arthur A. Hoy III, Charles Johns, Patrick Keefe,
Jamie LaCasse, Gregory Lockridge, Robert Louden,
Jack M. Mousseau, Scott Martin, Michael Miller, Gary
Morris, A. Chris Olson, Mark Rothman, Aleksandr
Sheykhet, James Sobey, Michael Stesney, Les Stuart,
Alexa Taylor, Thomas P. Theobald, Alexander
Thomé, Paul Tylar, Mark A. Wagner, Marilyn White,
Michael Wisneski, John C. Wurzenburger Jr
Building type: High-end residential
Structure: Post-tensioned slab
Exterior: Brick
Interior: Limestone, wood, gypsum, tiles, carpet,
glass
Gross square feet: 203,600

**New Inchon International Airport Passenger
Terminal Complex**
Design/Completion 1994/2000
Seoul, Republic of Korea
Korean Airports Authority
Principal in charge of design: Curtis W. Fentress
Principal in charge of production: James H.
Bradburn
Associate architects: Baum, Hi-Lim, Jung-Lim,
Wodushi Architects (BHJW); McClier Aviation
Group

Project architect: Jack M. Mousseau
Interior designer: Barbara K. Hochstetler
Project director: Thomas J. Walsh
Job captain: Richard Burkett
Design team: Galen Bailey, Todd R. Britton, Richard Burkett, John Gagnon, Arthur A. Hoy III, Anthia Kappos, Ned Kirschbaum, Lauren Lee, John M. McGahey, Wilbur Moore, Gary Morris, Brian Ostler, Michelle Ray, Tim Roush, Amy Solomon, Les Stuart, Michael O. Winters, John C. Wurzenberger Jr
Building type: Airport, train station
Structure: Steel frame, concrete
Exterior finish: Architectural precast concrete, glass, metal panel
Interior finish: Granite, paint, wood, stainless steel, architectural precast concrete
Gross square feet: 5,400,000
Number of floors: 6
Parking: 2,000 spaces

1995

One Wynkoop Plaza
Design/Completion 1995/1998
Denver, Colorado
Thermo Development Inc.
Principal in charge of design: Curtis W. Fentress
Principal in charge of production: James H. Bradburn
Associate architect: Shears-Leese Associated Architects
Project designer: Brian Chaffee
Design team: Catherine Dunn, Charles Johns
Building type: Multi-unit residential
Structure: Cast-in-place steel-reinforced concrete
Exterior: Brick, stone, metal, synthetic stucco
Interior: Tiles, wood, gypsum, carpet, glass
Gross square feet: 65,000

The Dunbar Resort
Design/Completion 1995/1998
Deadwood, South Dakota
The Dunbar Resort
Principal in charge of design: Curtis W. Fentress
Principal in charge of production: James H. Bradburn
Design architect: Hill/Glazier Architects Inc.
Project designer: Robert Glazier
Project manager: John M. Kudrycki
Design team: Warren Hogue III, Ned Kirschbaum, Robert Louden, Scott Martin, A. Chris Olson, Robert Riffle, Alexa Taylor, Thomas P. Theobald, Alexander Thomé
Building type: Hotel
Structure: Cast-in-place concrete, steel
Exterior: Stone, brick, cement board, metal
Interior: Wood, granite, brick, carpet
Gross square feet: 425,000

City of Oakland Administration Buildings
Design/Completion 1995/1998
Oakland, California
City of Oakland
Principal in charge of design: Curtis W. Fentress
Principal in charge of production: James H. Bradburn
Associate architects: Muller & Caulfield: Gerson/Overstreet
Project architect: Ronald R. Booth

Project designers: Ronald R. Booth, Peter D. Carlson, Catherine Dunn
Project manager: Jeff Olson
Interior Designer: Barbara Fentress
Design team: John Conklin, Gregory R. Gidez, Warren Hogue III, Kristen Hurty, Gregory Lockridge, Michael Miller, Jack M. Mousseau, Mark Outman, Trey Warren, Michael O. Winters, Jacqueline Wisniewski
Building type: Office buildings and parking garage
Structure: Steel
Exterior: Architectural precast concrete, glass
Interior: gypsum, carpet
Gross square feet: 450,000 (building); 100,000 (parking)

1996

Bentley Design Competition
Design 1996
Long Beach, California
The Rakovitch Company
Principal in charge of design: Curtis W. Fentress
Principal in charge of production: James H. Bradburn
Project designer: Deborah Lucking
Project manager: Mark Rothman
Design team: Petr Dostal, Cydney Fisher, Haia Ghalib, Ned Kirschbaum, Scott Martin, Mark McGlothlin
Building type: Multi-use development
Structure: Concrete
Exterior: Brick, masonry
Interior: Wood, carpet, glass
Gross square feet: 3,000,000

DIA Westin Hotel
Design 1996
Denver, Colorado
DIA Development Corporation
Principal in charge of design: Curtis W. Fentress
Principal in charge of production: James H. Bradburn
Design team: Brian Chaffee, James Sobey, Thomas J. Walsh
Building type: Hotel
Structure: Steel frame, precast concrete
Exterior: Architectural precast concrete, glass
Interior: Granite, stainless steel, gypsum, carpet, glass
Gross square feet: 325,000

ICG Communications Corporate Headquarters
Design/Completion 1996/1997
Englewood, Colorado
ICG Communications Inc.
Principal in charge of design: Curtis W. Fentress
Principal in charge of production: James H. Bradburn
Design architect: W. Stephen Wood
Project architect: Michael O. Winters
Project manager: John M. Kudrycki
Design team: William B. Buyers, Todd R. Britton, Robert Riffle, Alekandr Sheykhet, Amy Soloman, Alexander Thomé, Jacqueline Wisniewski
Building type: Corporate headquarters offices
Structure: Steel
Exterior: Granite, glass
Interior: Ceramic tiles, marble, metal, wood, carpet, glass
Gross square feet: 250,000

J.D. Edwards & Co. Corporate Headquarters
Design/Completion 1996/1997
Denver, Colorado
J.D. Edwards and Co.
Principal in charge of design: Curtis W. Fentress
Principal in charge of production: James H. Bradburn
Project designer: Ronald R. Booth
Project manager: Jeff Olson
Job captain: Robert Louden
Design team: Robin Ault, Garrett M. Christnacht, Haia Ghalib, David Harmon, Warren Hogue III, Sanjeev Molhatra, Robert Riffle, Alexander Thomé
Building type: Corporate headquarters offices
Structure: Steel frame, concrete core
Exterior: Architectural precast concrete, aluminum
Interior: Mahogany, granite, ceramic tiles, glass
Gross square feet: 216,000

Gulf Canada Resources Limited
Design/Completion 1996/1997
Denver, Colorado
Gulf Canada Resources Limited
Principals in charge of design: Curtis W. Fentress and Michael O. Winters
Principal in charge of production: James H. Bradburn
Project designer: Jamie LaCasse
Project manager: John C. Wurzenburger Jr
Design team: Todd R. Britton, Shannon Cody, Cydney Fisher, Ali Gidfar, David Harman, Patrick Keefe, Brent Mather, Mark McGlothlin, Irena Mokrova, Amy Soloman
Building type: Corporate headquarters offices
Interior: Wood, custom furnishings, glass
Gross square feet: 50,000

Regional Transportation Commission and Regional Flood Control District Headquarters and Administrative Center
Design/Completion 1996/1998
Las Vegas, Nevada
Regional Transportation Commission
Principal in charge of design: Michael O. Winters
Principal in charge of production: James H. Bradburn
Design team: Todd R. Britton, Robert Louden, Brent Mather, Sanjeev Malhotra, Robert Riffel, Amy Solomon
Building type: Govenmental headquarters offices
Structure: Steel frame, concrete core
Exterior: Sandstone, glass, painted metal
Interior: Granite, stucco, gypsum, carpet
Gross square feet: 70,000

Palmetto Bay Plantation Villas
Design/Completion 1996/1999
Camp Bay–Port Royal, Roatan, Honduras
Roatan Development Group
Principal in charge of design: Curtis W. Fentress
Principal in charge of production: James H. Bradburn
Project designer: James Sobey
Building type: Resort condominiums
Structures: Concrete, wood
Exterior: Concrete, wood
Interior: Tropical hardwood, gypsum, stone tiles
Gross square feet: 4,792,000

The New Doha International Airport
Design/Completion 1996/2000
Doha, Qatar
Ministry of Municipal Affairs and Agriculture
Principal in charge of design: Curtis W. Fentress
Principal in charge of production: James H.
Bradburn
Project designer: Jack M. Mousseau
Project manager: Ned Kirschbaum
Design team: Garrett M. Christnacht, Shannon Cody,
Jack Cook, Haia Ghalib, Gregory Lockridge,
Deborah Lucking, Scott Martin, Mark Outman,
Robert Riffle, Valerie Slack, Alexa Taylor, Thomas P.
Theobald, Alexander Thome', Jacqueline Wisniewski
Building type: Airport
Structure: Cast-in-place concrete, steel frame
Exterior: Plaster, glazed tiles
Interior: Plaster, granite, carpet
Gross square feet: 900,000

1997

Midway Office Complex and Master Plan
Design 1997
Memphis, Tennessee
Private corporation
Principal in charge of design: Curtis W. Fentress
Principal in charge of production: James H.
Bradburn
Design team: Ronald R. Booth, Cydney Fisher, Mark
McGlothlin
Building type: Corporate headquarters offices
Structure: Precast concrete
Exterior: Architectural precast concrete
Interior: Gypsum, carpet, glass
Gross square feet: 1,500,000

Kuala Lumpur Hotel and Office Complex
Design/Completion 1997/2000
Kuala Lumpur, Malaysia
Hiap Aik Construction Berhad
Principal in charge of design: Curtis W. Fentress
Principal in charge of production: James H.
Bradburn
Project designer: James Sobey
Project manager: Greg D. Billingham
Building type: Investment office building, hotel
Structure: Precast concrete
Exterior: Metal, glass
Interior: Wood, masonry, gypsum, carpet, glass
Gross square feet: 920,000

Presidio Town Center
Design/Completion 1997/2000
San Francisco, California
Bayshore Properties Inc.
Principal in charge of design: Curtis W. Fentress
Principal in charge of production: James H.
Bradburn
Project designer: James Sobey
Building type: Mixed-use development
Structure: Concrete
Exterior: Architectural precast concrete
Interior: Wood, masonry, carpet, glass
Gross square feet: 1,038,000

Larimer County Justice Center
Design/Completion 1997/2000
Fort Collins, Colorado
Larimer County Commissioners
Principal in charge of design: Curtis W. Fentress
Principal in charge of production: James H.
Bradburn
Project designer: Brian Chaffee
Building type: County courthouse
Structure: Structural steel, concrete
Exterior: Architectural precast concrete, brick,
stone, metal
Interior: Terrazzo, stone, wood, gypsum, carpet, glass
Gross square feet: 79,150

Goldrush Casino
Design/Completion 1997/2000
Central City, Colorado
Dynasty Corporation Hotel and Casino
Principal in charge of design: Curtis W. Fentress
Principal in charge of production: James H.
Bradburn
Project manager: Jack Cook
Design team: Arthur A. Hoy III, Jack M. Mousseau
Building type: Casino
Structure: Steel, concrete
Exterior: Stone, wood, metal roofing, metal siding
Interior: Plaster, carpet, tiles
Gross square feet: 60,000

Deira Bus Station and Car Park
Design/Completion 1997/2000
Dubai, United Arab Emirates
Dubai Municipality
Principal in charge of design: Curtis W. Fentress
Principal in charge of production: James H.
Bradburn
Associate architect: Dar Al-Handasah Shair and
Partners
Project designer: Brian Chaffee
Design team: William B. Buyers, Deborah Lucking
Building type: Multi-modal, mixed-use
transportation terminus
Structure: Steel, concrete
Exterior: Concrete, tiles, ornamental metal
Interior: Tiles, concrete, plaster, wood
Gross square feet: 944,881

Blackhawk Casino
Design/Completion TBD
Black Hawk, Colorado
Riviera Hotel
Principal in charge of design: Curtis W. Fentress
Principal in Charge of Production: James H.
Bradburn
Project manager: Brian Chaffee
Design team: TBD
Building type: Casino
Structure: Steel, concrete
Exterior: Stone, wood, metal roofing, metal siding
Interior: Plaster, carpet, tiles
Gross square feet: 60,000
Parking: 500 spaces

Selected Awards and Competitions

Firm Awards

Firm of the Year
Western Mountain Region, American
Institute of Architects
1996

Firm of the Year
Colorado Chapter, American Institute
of Architects
1994

Selected National Citations

Design-Build Excellence Award
Design-Build Institute of America
Natural Resources Building
1997

Award of Honor
United States Department of
Transportation
Denver International Airport Passenger
Terminal Complex
1995

Award of Citation
American Association of School
Administrators (AASA)
University of Colorado Mathematics
Building and Gemmill Engineering
Sciences Library
1993

Citation for Excellence
American Institute of Architects
Architecture for Justice Exhibition
Jefferson County Government Center
1990

AIA Awards

Award of Honor
Western Mountain Region, American
Institute of Architects
Clark County Government Center
1997

Honorable Mention
Colorado Chapter, American Institute
of Architects
National Museum of Wildlife Art
1996

Award of Merit
Colorado Chapter, American Institute of
Architects
Natural Resources Laboratory and
Administration Building
1996

Award of Honor
Western Mountain Region, American
Institute of Architects
National Museum of Wildlife Art
1996

Award of Honor
Denver Chapter, American Institute
of Architects
National Museum of Wildlife Art
1996

Award of Distinction
People's Choice
Denver Chapter, American Institute
of Architects
National Museum of Wildlife Art
1996

Award of Distinction
Denver Chapter, American Institute
of Architects
Dinosaur Discovery Museum
1996

Award of Distinction
People's Choice
Denver Chapter, American Institute
of Architects
National Museum of Wildlife Art
1995

Award of Merit
Denver Chapter, American Institute
of Architects
University of Colorado Mathematics
Building and Gemmill Engineering
Sciences Library
1994

Award of Honor
Western Mountain Region, American
Institute of Architects
Denver International Airport Passenger
Terminal Complex
1994

Award of Honor
Denver Chapter, American Institute
of Architects
Denver International Airport Passenger
Terminal Complex
1994

Award of Honor
Colorado Chapter, American Institute
of Architects
Denver International Airport Passenger
Terminal Complex
1994

Award of Merit
Architecture and Energy
Portland Chapter, American Institute
of Architects
Natural Resources Laboratory and
Administration Building
1993

Design Award
Northern Colorado Chapter, American
Institute of Architects
Leanin Tree Gallery
1992

Design Award
Colorado Chapter, American Institute
of Architects
Kittredge Building
1992

Design Award
Colorado Chapter, American Institute
of Architects
Ronstadt Transit Center
1991

Award of Merit
Western Mountain Region, American
Institute of Architects
Ronstadt Transit Center
1991

Award of Merit
Western Mountain Region, American
Institute of Architects
Black American West Museum
1991

Award of Merit
Denver Chapter, American Institute
of Architects
Ronstadt Transit Center
1991

Award of Merit
Denver Chapter, American Institute
of Architects
Jefferson County Human Services Building
1991

Award of Merit
Denver Chapter, American Institute
of Architects
Denver Permit Center
1991

Award of Merit
Denver Chapter, American Institute of
Architects
Black American West Museum
1991

Award of Honor
Western Mountain Region, American
Institute of Architects
Jefferson County Human Services Building
1991

Award of Honor
Denver Chapter, American Institute of
Architects
Colorado Convention Center
1991

Award of Merit
Western Mountain Region, American
Institute of Architects
Colorado Convention Center
1990

Award of Merit
Colorado Chapter, American Institute
of Architects
1999 Broadway
1990

Award of Honor
Kansas Chapter, American Institute
of Architects
Museum of Western Art
1990

Award of Honor
Colorado Chapter, American Institute
of Architects
Colorado Convention Center
1990

Award of Merit
Colorado Chapter, American Institute
of Architects
Denver Permit Center
1989

Award of Excellence in Architecture
Western Mountain Region, American
Institute of Architects
Denver Permit Center
1989

Award of Merit
Denver Chapter, American Institute
of Architects
Odd Fellows Hall
1988

Award of Honor
Denver Chapter, American Institute
of Architects
Museum of Western Art
1987

Award of Merit
Western Mountain Region, American
Institute of Architects
One DTC
1986

Design Award
Colorado Chapter, American Institute
of Architects
Odd Fellows Hall
1985

Award of Honor
Western Mountain Region, American
Institute of Architects
Museum of Western Art
1985

Award of Honor
Western Mountain Region, American
Institute of Architects
1999 Broadway
1985

Award of Honor
Denver Chapter, American Institute
of Architects
Museum of Western Art
1985

Award of Honor
Best of Show
Denver Chapter, American Institute
of Architects
Museum of Western Art
1985

Design Award
Colorado Chapter, American Institute
of Architects
Museum of Western Art
1984

Award of Merit
Western Mountain Region, American
Institute of Architects
Odd Fellows Hall
1984

Community Awards

National Preservation Honor Award
National Trust for Historic Preservation
Perry's Egyptian Theater Renovation
1997

Interior Design Giant
Interior Design Magazine
1991

Architect of the Year
American Subcontractors Association
of Colorado
1991

Award of Achievement
Professional Engineers of Colorado
1990

Ten Most Distinguished
Denver Business Magazine
1985

Young Professional of the Year
Building Design & Construction Magazine
1981

Winning Competition Entries

Larimer County Justice Center
Fort Collins, Colorado
1997

New Doha International Airport
Doha, Qatar
1996

Bentley Design Competition
Long Beach, California
1996

City of Oakland Administration Buildings
Oakland, California
1995

**Howard Hughes Corporation Corporate
Headquarters**
Las Vegas, Nevada
1995

**New Inchon International Airport
Passenger Terminal Complex**
Seoul, Republic of Korea
1992

Clark County Government Center
Las Vegas, Nevada
1992

National Cowboy Hall of Fame
Oklahoma City, Oklahoma
1991

**Natural Resources Laboratory and
Administration Building**
Olympia, Washington
1989

Colorado Convention Center
Denver, Colorado
1987

**Data General Field Engineering Logistics
Center**
Fountain, Colorado
1984

Selected Bibliography

Fentress Bradburn Architects

"$24.2 Million Idaho Power Plan Gets 'OK'." *The Idaho Statesman* (1996).

"Access Approved." *Passenger Management International* (October 1997).

"Against the Odds." *Landscape Architecture* (April 1996).

"An American in Qatar." *l'Arca* (October 1996).

"Architecture and Energy Building Excellence in the Northwest: 1993 Design Awards." *Architecture* (vol. 82, no. 5, May 1993), p. 113.

Arnaboldi, Mario Antonio. "Airport on the Water." *l'Arca* (no. 71, May 1993), pp. 24–29.

Berger, Horst. "Modern Basilica." *Fabrics in Architecture* (vol. 5, no. 3, May/June 1993), pp. 10–21.

"Blueprints for Success." *Colorado Business Magazine* (November 1997).

Brown, Daniel C. "Reviving an Architectural Pioneer." *Building Design and Construction* (vol. 24, no. 10, October 1983), pp. 40–43.

"C.W. Fentress and Associates: Denver Landmark: Odd Fellows Hall." *Interiors* (vol. 142, no. 9, April 1983), p. 22.

"C.W. Fentress Designs Denver's Reliance Center." *Architectural Record* (vol. 170, no. 4, March 1982), p. 41.

Canty, Donald. "Building with a Checkered Past Renovated as a Museum." *Architecture* (vol. 75, no. 11, November 1986), pp. 78–79.

Cattaneo, Renato. "A Canopied Air Terminal." *l'Arca* (no. 73, July/August 1993), pp. 19–23.

Chalmers, Ray. "Mullion-free Exterior Enhances Office Views: Four-sided Structural Silicone Glazing First in the Rocky Mountain Region." *Building Design and Construction* (vol. 25, no. 3, March 1984), pp. 176–179.

Chandler, Roger A. *Fentress Bradburn Architects*. Washington, DC: Studio Press, 1995.

Chandler, Roger A. "Learning from Las Vegas? The Clark County Government Center." *Competitions 2* (Winter 1992), pp. 31–39.

Chandler, Roger A. "Variations on a Theme: Americans Win Airport Competitions on the Pacific Rim." *Competitions 3* (Summer 1993), pp. 30–39.

Cohen, Edie. "Curtis Fentress: The Architect Restricts Intervention in an Historically Significant Denver House." *Interior Design* (vol. 65, no. 4, March 1994), pp. 112–115.

"Colorado Trends." *Intermountian Architecture* (Fall 1994).

Continuum. Bentley Publications, November 1997.

"Convention Center Offers Dramatic Design." *Sun Coast Architect–Builder* (vol. 56, no. 11, November 1991), pp. W28–30.

Cooper, Jerry. "Balboa Company: Fifty-seven Floors above the Mile-High City: C.W. Fentress and Associates Creates Art-inspired Corporate Offices for a Denver Investor." *Interior Design* (vol. 58, no. 10, August 1987), pp. 188–192.

"Curtis Fentress with Stanley Collyer." *Competitions* (Fall 1995).

"Curtis Worth Fentress." *Denver Business Journal* (vol. 13, no. 4, December 1985), p. 23.

Curtis Worth Fentress. Milan: l'Arca Edizioni, 1995.

"Curved Complex Conveys Distinctive Civic Character." *Building Design and Construction* (December 1994).

Della Corte, Evelyn. "The Museum of Western Art: The Interiors of Denver's Newest Museum Win 1984 ASID Project Design Award." *Interior Design* (vol. 55, no. 10, October 1984), pp. 204–209.

"Democracy in the Desert." *Facilities Design and Management* (January 1997).

"Denver Airport Design Unveiled: The Terminal Will Be Capped by One of the Nation's Largest Cable Supported Fabric Roofs." *Building Design and Construction* (vol. 32, no. 1, January 1991), p. 17.

"Denver International Airport." *l'Arca* (November 1994).

"Denver International Airport." *The Consultant* (Summer 1996).

"Denver Permit Center, Denver, Colorado." *New Mexico Architecture* (vol. 31, no. 3/4, May–August 1990), p. 17.

"Denver's New Airport Flying High." *San Francisco Chronicle* (March 1997).

"Denver: Take a Closer Look." *Fortune* (vol. 127, no. 8, April 19, 1993), pp. 164–172.

Dietsch, Deborah K. "Green Realities: Architects Must Agree on Standards To Distinguish the Green from the Faux." *Architecture* (vol. 83, no. 6, June 1993), p. 15.

"Easy Breathing in Washington." *Facilities Design and Management* (May 1993).

Eng, Rick. "1999 Broadway Establishes Harmony between Skyscraper and Sanctuary." *Designers West* (vol. 33, no. 6, April 1986), pp. 86–87.

"Fentress Bradburn's Winning Ways Aid Growth." *Ascent* (Spring 1994).

"Fentress Bradburn Wins Design Competition." *MSM* (August 1996).

Fentress, Curtis Worth. "Architect Explains Design Goals of New Colorado Convention Center." *Denver Post* (June 18, 1990), p. B7.

Fentress, Curtis Worth. "Convention Center Took its Model from Future." *Rocky Mountain News* (June 18, 1990), p. 44.

Fentress, Curtis Worth. "Design Intelligence." *Sun Belt Buildings Journal* (vol. 9, no. 12, April 1985), p. 7.

Fentress, Curtis Worth. "Doughnut Hole Can Coexist in City Plan." *Rocky Mountain News* (April 30, 1983), p. N32.

Fentress, Curtis Worth. "Preservation Requires Skill." *Rocky Mountain News* (January 31, 1984), p. B29.

Fentress, Curtis Worth & Weingardt, Richard. "One Denver Tech Center: Commanding Views of Earth and Sky." *Modern Steel Construction* (vol. 27, no. 6, November/December 1987), pp. 23–27.

"Firm of the Year: Fentress Bradburn." *The Daily Journal* (December 1994).

Fisher, Thomas. "Projects: Flights of Fantasy." *Progressive Architecture* (vol. 73, no. 3, March 1992), pp. 105–107.

"The Forgotten and the Serene." *Open Spaces* (March 1995).

"Form or Function." *Las Vegas Sun* (July 1993).

"Frankly Speaking: Curt Fentress and Jim Bradburn Talk about the Practice of Architecture." *Daily Journal* (vol. 94, no. 44, July 24, 1990): s. 2, pp. 11–12.

"The Government Center that Came in on Budget." *Facilities Design and Management* (May 1994).

"Gunter Hall Renovation." *Historic Resource Facilities* (Summer 1997).

Hardenbaugh, Don (comp.). *Retrospective of Courthouse Design 1980–1991.* Williamsburg, Va: National Center for State Courts, 1992, pp. 64–65.

Harriman, Marc S. "Designing for Daylight." *Architecture* (vol. 81, no. 10, October 1992), p. 89.

Henderson, Justin. "Convening Comfortably: C.W. Fentress J.H. Bradburn and Associates Humanize the Overscale in the New Colorado Convention Center." *Interiors* (vol. 150, no. 12, July 1991), pp. 44–49.

Henderson, Justin. "For the People: Accessibility Inspires the Master Plan for the Jefferson County Municipal Center by C.W. Fentress J. H. Bradburn and Associates." *Interiors* (vol. 150, no. 12, July 1991), pp. 50–51.

"How an Unusual Site Influenced Architecture." *Building Design and Construction* (vol. 21, no. 10, October 1980), pp. 56–57.

"ICG Builds Denver Headquarters." *Colorado Real Estate Journal* (October–November 1996).

"International Design Competition: The New Seoul Metropolitan Airport Passenger Terminal." *Architecture and Environment* (no. 101, January 1993), pp. 123–171.

"Is This Any Way To Build an Airport?" *Architectural Record* (November 1994).

"J.D. Edwards Boots Up at DTC." *Colorado Real Estate Journal* (November 1996).

"Jefferson County Human Services." *Progressive Architecture* (vol. 74, no. 3, March 1993), pp. 42–43.

Justice Facilities Review. American Institute of Architects, 1997–98.

Kania, Alan. "C.W. Fentress J.H. Bradburn and Associates Celebrating Ten-year Anniversary." *Daily Journal* (vol. 94, no. 44, July 24, 1990): s. 2, pp. 1–2.

Landecker, Heidi. "Airport Departures." *Architecture* (vol. 82, no. 8, August 1993), pp. 42–45.

"Leaving 'Las Vegas'." *Contract Design* (February 1997).

Loebelson, Andrew. "The Second 100 Interior Design Giants of 1991." *Interior Design* (vol. 62, no. 10, July 1991), pp. 49–64.

Maluga, Mark J. "Denver Permit Center: Fast-track Facelift Classically Revitalizes a 1960's Structure." *Building Design and Construction* (vol. 31, no. 11, November 1990), pp. 62–65.

"Manca Titolo." *l'Arca* (1992).

"Mile High Magnificence." *Hemispheres* (October 1993).

"National Cowboy Hall of Fame." *l'Arca* (April 1995).

"National Wildlife Museum." *l'Arca* (February 1997).

"The Natural Resources Building in Olympia Washington." *l'Arca* (May 1994).

"A New Financial Center in Tucson Draws on the Mission Style." *Interiors* (vol. 146, no. 4, November 1986), p. 40.

"New Seoul Metropolitan Airport." *Progressive Architecture* (vol. 74, no. 3, March 1993), p. 25.

"Now, An Airport You Can Love?" *Condé Nast Traveler* (October 1994).

Oliszewicz, B. Ann. "Young Professionals Competition." *Building Design and Construction* (vol. 21, no. 10, October 1980), pp. 54–55.

"Olympia's Natural Resources Building." *Architectural Record* (vol. 178, no. 12, November 1990), p. 15.

"On the Boards: Natural Resources Building, Olympia, Washington: C.W. Fentress J.H. Bradburn and Associates." *Architecture* (vol. 80, no. 5, May 1991), p. 48.

"On the Horizon: Denver Architects and Their Work: C.W. Fentress." *Colorado Homes and Lifestyles* (vol. 5, no. 2, March/April 1985), pp. 42–45.

"The Other Las Vegas." *Architecture* (April 1996).

"Pencil Points: Shades of Saint Barts." *Progressive Architecture* (vol. 64, no. 10, October 1983), p. 49.

Pierson, John. "Denver Airport Rises under Gossamer Roof." *Wall Street Journal* (vol. 127, no. 99, November 17, 1992), Western edition, p. B1.

"Poetry in Motion." *The Architectural Review* (February 1995).

"Projects in Progress." *Sun Coast Architect–Builder* (vol. 47, no. 8, August 1982), p. 26.

Rebeck, Gene. "Monumental Potential." *Fabrics in Architecture* (vol. 4, no. 4, July/August 1992), p. 16.

"Regional Pride." *Architecture* (May 1995).

"Restoration Revives Architectural Character yet Permits Modern Styling." *Sun Coast Architect–Builder* (vol. 53, no. 5, May 1988), pp. 38–39.

"Rethinking Urban Infrastructure." *Architecture* (August 1994).

"Revitalizing the Excitement of Travel." *Passenger Terminal World* (1995).

Russell, James S. "Height + Water = Cool." *Architectural Record* (vol. 180, no. 8, August 1992), pp. 40–41.

"Saving Grace: The Survival of Holy Ghost Church in Denver, Colorado Is Secured by Development." *Interiors* (vol. 141, no. 10, May 1982), p. 22.

Shaman, Diane. "Seeking Remedies for Indoor Air Pollution Problems." *New York Times* (April 12, 1992), s. 1, pp. 0, 13.

"The Shrine to Western Wildlife." *New York Times* (January 1995).

"Sloped Terraces for an Office Building in Denver, Colorado." *L'Industria Italiana del Cemento* (no. 651, January 1991), pp. 38–46.

"Spotlight: Museums." *Facility Manager* (October 1993).

"Stazione degli autobus." *Costruire In Laterizio* (August 1997).

Stein, Karen D. "Snow-capped Symbol." *Architectural Record* (vol. 181, no. 6, June 1993), pp. 106–107.

"Thin Sheets of Air." *Progressive Architecture* (vol. 66, no. 6, June 1985), pp. 104–110.

"Transit Center Provides Oasis of Comfort for Bus Passengers." *Sun Coast Architect–Builder* (vol. 58, no. 5, May 1993), pp. W2–W3.

"Tucson Bank Tower Suggests Influence of Spanish Missions." *Buildings Design Journal* (vol. 3, no. 9, September 1985), p. 8.

Walker, Diane N. (ed.) *American Architecture: The State of the Art in the 80's.* Ashland, Ky: Hanover Publishing Company, 1985, pp. 10–11, 132–133.

Weingardt, Richard. "Colorado Architecture: The Best Buildings of the Modern Age." *Colorado Business Magazine* (vol. 17, no. 2, February 1990), pp. 38–43.

Weingardt, Richard & Rundles, Jeff. "Magnificent Colorado Structures Never Built." *Colorado Business Magazine* (vol. 19, no. 2, February 1992), pp. 41–44.

"Wild Things." *Denver Post Magazine* (September 1994).

"Young Jong Island: New International Airport Design Competition." *Architectural Culture* (no. 140, January 1993), pp. 204–213.